GANDHI

GANDHI

The Traditional
Roots of
Charisma

Susanne Hoeber Rudolph
and Lloyd I. Rudolph

The University of Chicago Press
Chicago and London

This book originally appeared as part
two of *The Modernity of Tradition:
Political Development in India.*

**The University of Chicago Press,
Chicago 60637**

**The University of Chicago Press,
Ltd., London**

© 1967, 1983 by The University of
    Chicago
All rights reserved. Published 1967
Paperback edition 1983
Printed in the United States of
    America

00 99 98 97 96 95 94 93 92 91   5 6 7 8 9 10

**Library of Congress Cataloging in
Publication Data**

Rudolph, Susanne Hoeber.
   Gandhi, the traditional roots of
   charisma.

   Originally published as part 2 of the
Modernity of Tradition by Lloyd I.
Rudolph and Susanne Hoeber Rudolph.
   1. Leadership.   2. Gandhi,
Mahatma, 1869–1948.   3. Politics,
Practical—Psychological aspects.
4. Courage.   5. Self-control.
I. Rudolph, Lloyd I.   II. Rudolph,
Lloyd I. Modernity of tradition.
III. Title.
HM141.R8   1983   303.3′4   83–1179
ISBN 0–226–73136–7

CONTENTS

PREFACE

Our interpretation of Gandhi was formed between the mid-1950s and the mid-1960s, the decade between decolonization and the Vietnam War and fifteen years before the victory in Iran of Islamic revivalism. It was widely believed at the time that "new nations" had to break with—even repudiate—tradition to become modern. Ancient civilizations were not so much dangerous as decadent. Scholars and statesmen talked of stages of development, take-off, and the prerequisites of democracy.

Our interpretation of Gandhi expressed a countercurrent. We called the larger work in which this account of Gandhi first appeared *The Modernity of Tradition* because we found that social change in India involved adaptation of its past inheritance as much as it did the destruction and displacement of that inheritance. India's indeterminant future, it seemed, was being shaped by civilizational continuities and affinities. We did not find this necessarily dangerous or undesirable and we tried to show why.

Gandhi, who describes himself in his autobiography as descended from a caste of petty merchants and was in fact the son and grandson of princely state prime ministers, became for Indians *bapu* (father) and *Mahatma* (great soul). How was this possible? How was it done? We find the answers in the traditional roots of his charisma, the subtitle we have given this book. Max Weber, who gave currency to the concept of charisma, found that charismatic leadership arose spontaneously and moved history in hitherto unlikely and even unanticipated directions. Charismatic leadership was a wild card that reordered the values contained in the deck of extant historical determinants. For us, Gandhi's charismatic leadership was itself in part historically determined, rooted in the aspects of tradition he interpreted for his time. Gandhi's revitalization of tradition involved breaks with its entrenched values, practices, and interests: his struggle against untouchability as a world view and social practice; his insistence on the dignity of all callings and the work they entail; and his transformation of the Indian National Congress from a body narrowly concerned with the interests of an anglicized elite to a socially concerned mass organization. In pursuing these and other transformations of Indian character, society, and politics he used traditional symbols and language to convey new meanings and to reconstitute social action.

Gandhi realized in his daily life and his public actions cultural ideals that many Indians honored in their own lives but could not themselves enact. He and his followers shared, for example, the traditional Hindu belief that a person's capacity for self-control enhanced his capacity to control his environment. This was the key to Gandhi's political potency. In a self-fulfilling prophecy of mutual expectations and recognitions, Gandhi and those to whom he spoke believed that the more he could realize the cultural ideal of ascetic self-control over enslaving or destructive passions, the more qualified he became as their leader.

Gandhi's "experiments with truth," the title of his autobiography, never ceased. One result of his experiments was a self-critical, ethical, and inclusive nationalism. Gandhi frequently spoke of *swaraj* (literally *swa* "self" and *raj* "rule"), a word derived from Sanskrit and common to many Indian languages. He used its double meaning, rule thyself and national self-rule, to teach by example and precept that Indians would not be ready for or capable of national independence until they had reformed themselves and their society.

Gandhi's nationalism achieved an ethical universalism that attracted—and still attracts—attention and followers outside India. It was able to do so because Gandhi placed right means (such as nonviolence) above desired ends. He instructed a generation that nonviolent resistance was a transforming and agentic force rather than a passive tactic of the weak. To protest injustice without hatred and violence required moral and physical courage. Gandhi showed that resolving conflicts by appealing to shared values and interests could replace enmity with community. He depicted truth as a goal rather than as an archetype or a revelation and compared it to a diamond whose many facets exposed a variety of meanings. Because Gandhi gave truth a contextual and experimental form, it could be found in all faiths and realized in the lives of all men.

GANDHI

In an era that takes matters of religious faith lightly, it is difficult to consider a man who is suspected of saintliness. The task is particularly vexing for Americans whose origins in flight from Europe and its feudal legacies mute their memories of a time when saints were important people. Was Gandhi's political shrewdness compatible with the essential innocence of heart that one asks of saints? A generation of ambivalent skeptics in one breath denies that saints exist and in the next avers that Gandhi could not have been one because he did not meet such and such criterion of saintliness. For us, Gandhi's meaning and contribution can best be explored outside the framework of saintliness.

Whether Gandhi did or did not speed Britain's exit from India provides another distraction. It can plausibly be argued that Britain would have departed from the subcontinent in or about 1947 whether or not Gandhi occupied the historical stage. A review of Gandhi's role in gaining the political objective of Indian independence fails to touch what may prove to be his most important contribution, what he did for Indian character and capacities. Gandhi's leadership, regardless of its objective success or failure, had important subjective consequences, repairing wounds in self-esteem inflicted by generations of imperial subjection, restoring courage and potency, recruiting and mobilizing new constituencies and leaders, helping India to acquire national coherence.

That Gandhi should have been one of the most conspicuous modernizers of Indian politics suggests that some elements of tradition can serve modern functions. Indian history exhibits great variety in the realm of non-Kshatriya leadership, from the Brahmanic teacher addressing himself to a limited elite in an esoteric medium (Sanskrit) to the *bhakti* (devotional) teacher communicating with popular audiences through familiar symbols and local languages. If the

3

Sanskritic and textual bias of Indology placed the first mode in the foreground of scholarly and world perspectives of India, the second is today becoming more visible as a result of a new Indology that looks beyond Sanskrit texts and of the replacement in Indian historiography of an elite by a democratic bias. Gandhi came from an area and family strongly influenced by bhakti. His identification with it shaped his political style and helped him, in the face of the limitations imposed by illiteracy and the dearth of mass communications, to do what great bhakti teachers for centuries past had done, to reach mass audiences by peripatetic teaching throughout the subcontinent.

Gandhi's commitment to non-violence and truth (satyagraha, or "truth force"), too, suggests how traditional ideals can be transformed for modern purposes. He self-consciously rejected the fatalistic, otherworldly, and ritualistic orientation that some Jain and Hindu practioners had lent them. His private struggle for competence and potency taught him to evoke their humanistic, evangelical, and world-mastering implications. If his commitments to non-violence and satyagraha had instrumental dimensions, fitting the requirements of an unarmed nation confronting an imperial conscience capable of responding to moral appeals, he infused their practice with meanings that transcend utility and national boundaries.

Gandhi's concern to rationalize and extend the organizational bases of Indian political life and his capacity to use efficiently himself, time, and resources were rooted in a Hindu expression of this-worldly asceticism. Here again a component of tradition functioned in a modern manner, helping Gandhi to master or manufacture his political environment. Like his political style and commitments to truth and non-violence, Gandhi's this-worldly asceticism arose out of the interaction between the religious and secular culture of family, community, and region and the psychological circumstances of a particular life. Like the religious asceticism required for virtue and potency, it found expression in his sense of vocation: "For me there is no distinction between politics and religion."[1] ". . . When I say that I prize my own salvation above everything else," he wrote, ". . . it does not mean that my personal salvation requires a sacrifice of

[1] "Interview to the 'Bombay Chronicle,' *The Bombay Chronicle,* February 18, 1922," in *Collected Works of Mahatma Gandhi* (Delhi, 1958——), XXII, 404.

India's political . . . salvation. But it implies that the two go together."[2]

Gandhi contributed to Indian political modernization too by asserting in example and precept a public ethic against the standards of private obligation to friends and family. In doing so, he translated into indigenous terms the civility that British law and administration brought to India by imbuing it with the moral remorselessness associated with the traditional practice of virtue and by applying it in traditional contexts.

Gandhi's leadership helps to illuminate the dynamics and particulars of charismatic leadership. Because signs of grace feature as an essential but transcendent aspect of charisma its human meaning is hard to fathom. Gandhi's doubts about his worthiness arose from the idiosyncratic circumstances of his psychological development. His uncertainty helped generate the energy and ideas that he invested in a personal quest for competence, meaning, and integrity. Drawing upon the social and historical resources that surrounded his life path, he fashioned an identity and a message that spoke to the experiences and problems of Indians living under foreign imperial subjection. The saliency and resonance of these personal solutions enabled them to be translated into public and historical ones. If he remained uncertain until the end about his worthiness, he yet perceived a relationship between his attempts at perfection, on the one hand, and the course of history and his public reception, on the other.

Gandhi's charisma had a cultural referent. His effectiveness as a peripatetic teacher was related less to his oratorical or theatrical skills —he never became a great speaker—than to the reputation that preceded him and the ideal that he embodied. The authenticity with which he sought virtue and the highest religious goals through self-control, truth, and non-violence re-enacted a familiar but rarely realized cultural model, that of the saintly man. By communicating in a fresh and historically relevant manner the idea that those who could master themselves could achieve serenity, religious merit, and mastery of their environment, he evoked a response that his authority as a consummate and skilled politician could not alone have commanded.

[2] "No End to My Sorrows," *Young India,* February 23, 1922, in *ibid.,* p. 462.

The ideological need to relate national identity and self-esteem to indigenous cultural traditions has lost urgency with the demise of the imperial power. As Gandhi's ideals and methods have faded among Indian generations more interested in economic development, social mobility, and national security, they have traveled abroad. Freed from their particular cultural and national setting, they can be found particularly in the United States where Martin Luther King has translated them for use in the struggle by American Negroes for equal rights and opportunities. Their continuing relevance in these and other circumstances suggests in yet another way how the opposition of modernity and tradition may obscure more than it clarifies processes of social change and political development.

The Fear of Cowardice

Like many thinkers and actors in the Indian tradition, Gandhi cared more for man's inner environment than his outer and was highly self-conscious about his effect on how Indians felt about themselves. The young Nehru, who often questioned the Mahatma's political strategy and tactics, concedes again and again his effect on the nationalist generation:

> Much that he said we only partially accepted or sometimes did not accept at all. But all this was secondary. The essence of his teaching was fearlessness and truth and action allied to these. . . . So, suddenly as it were, that black pall of fear was lifted from the people's shoulders, not wholly, of course, but to an amazing degree. . . . It was a psychological change, almost as if an expert in psychoanalytic method had probed deep into the patient's past, found out the origins of his complexes, exposed them to his view, and thus rid him of that burden.[1]

[1] Jawaharlal Nehru, *The Discovery of India* (New York, 1946), pp. 361–62.

The portrait of Gandhi probing the nation's historical subconscious is a telling one. Gandhi had a unique sensibility both for the nightmare terrors of the Indian psyche and for its commonplace daytime self-doubts. He understood both the fundamental fear of Indians that those Britons who judged them as lacking in basic components of moral worth—like courage—might be right and the more superficial doubts about their technical ability to do anything about removing the raj. The nightmare fears he understood in part by analogy with his own personal terrors, terrors involving especially the issue of courage. The shape that he gave to the national movement, above all the technique of satyagraha, had much more than strategic significance; it provided a path for action that "solved" some problems of Indian self-esteem arising from acceptance of the negative judgments of Englishmen.

One result of British rule had been to strengthen the appearance and reality of non-violent cultural norms. By the middle of the nineteenth century the last vestiges of organized Indian military power had sunk from view. Kshatriya rule and culture, particularly after 1858, lost their violent capabilities and concerns. Under the sheltering umbrella of British guarantees, ceremony and conspicuous consumption atrophied the will and diverted the resources of India's fighting classes. Even while British rule was making clear that Indians lacked power, it strengthened the non-violent dimensions of Indian culture by providing educational and related service opportunities that required the skills and temperament of the office rather than the scepter and sword. Adherence to non-violence, while conspicuous among the qualifications for reaching the eschatological goals of Sanskritic Hinduism, is only one of the social ideologies found in traditional thought. Violence, too, has occupied an important place in thought and history and has its share of legitimizing religious and secular norms. But as the psychological and moral effects of Britain's conquest and subjection of India spread and deepened, and Indians adapted to the roles the empire required, both Britons and Indians began to believe that non-violence and the corollaries the British attributed to it—passivity, weakness, and cowardice—were the norms of Indian culture and character. The belief led many Britons to think that the superiority of British power and culture was an inherent rather than a historical phenomenon. India's military heritage, the heroes and social ideology that legitimized the use of violence and the character and rule of those who practiced it were, if not forgotten, at least moved into the background. Within the literary heritage of Indian civilization the texts sanctioning the authority and sanctifying the norms of the non-martial twice-born received the lion's share of scholarly and official attention. This image of India survived the sufficiently violent if disorganized and politically unproductive events of the 1857 Rebellion and the partition agitation of 1905. It was out of such circumstances and materials that the British constructed the unsystematic theory of imperialism that legitimized and explained British domination and Indian subjection.

The things that Britons had to say about India varied so widely that any attempt to distil their judgments seems presumptuous. And yet, in the second half of the nineteenth century and at the turning of the twentieth, even as the nationalist movement was gathering strength and even as new policy decisions by Britons carried India farther toward self-government, distinctive themes in British judgments of India emerged. These judgments distinguished between certain categories of Indians, especially between "masculine" and "feminine" races, between the "natural" Indian leaders and the unrepresentative babus ("clerks") "posing" as leaders, and between the "real" Indians and the assimilated ones. In each case, the categories carried within themselves implications as to who was and was not with the angels. These themes are to be found more in the pronouncements of men like Lytton, Fitzjames Stephen, John Strachey, and Curzon, who were hostile to Indian self-rule, than Ripon or Allen Octavian Hume, who were sanguine on the same topic.

The distinction between masculine and feminine races is an especially pervasive theme in this unsystematic imperialist theory and appeared most frequently in connection with the Bengalis, whom most Englishmen knew best and who had most swiftly responded to English culture. The late Joseph Schumpeter remarked in his account of imperialism that many imperialists were feudal atavisms, men whose hunger for the chivalric life could not be accommodated by the middle-class civilization of nineteenth-century Europe and who turned to the new frontiers of the colonies for the challenge they could not find at home.[2] The picture one has of the precompetition wallahs, the early nineteenth-century English in India, clodhopping Collectors, trusty rifles slung over their shoulders, boar spears in their left hands, confirms this view.[3] Such men felt impatience with the allegedly unathletic Bengalis, and admiration for the muscular and venturesome tribal people of the Northwest. Although many came for reasons less romantic than feudal nostalgia, because of family traditions or interest in a remunerative and respectable career, and although many pursued timid Victorian and bureaucratic life styles rather than feudal virtues, practitioners of the swashbuckling style shaped the dominant image of Englishmen in India and, by contrast, the mirror image of Indians.

When Kipling, sedentary ideologue of the swashbuckling style, rhymed his verse and found that "East is East and West is West, and never the twain shall meet," he added that there was, however, *one* equalizer of national difference: courage. The frontier Pathan and the English soldier of his ballad could understand one another as warriors: "But there is neither East nor West, Border, nor Breed, nor Birth/When two strong men stand face to face, though they come from the ends of the earth."[4] Englishmen fancied, though, that this leveling element was available only among a limited number of Indians.

By the second half of the century, venturesome Englishmen went to Africa as often as to India; and if men of Strachey's and Curzon's era speak with contempt of Bengali "feminism," it is as much with the ambivalent masculinity produced by *fin de siècle* British public school training as with the knowledge gained from experience with Bengali character. There is an empirical basis for their perception. Much of Indian society, particularly that part made up of the nonmartial twice-born castes, does seem to tolerate a larger component

[2] Joseph Schumpeter, "The Sociology of Imperialism," in *Social Classes and Imperialism,* trans. Heinz Norden and Paul Sweezy (New York, 1951), pp. 65–98.

[3] Philip Woodruff's two volume work, *The Men Who Ruled India* (London, 1953–54), admirably develops this picture.

[4] Rudyard Kipling, "The Ballad of East and West," in *Rudyard Kipling's Verse* (New York, 1940), p. 233.

of feminine qualities in its men than most Western societies do, even while homosexuality appears to be a less significant issue in India than in more "masculine" countries.[5] The differences in cultural patterning were sharpened by the compulsions of roles. Occupying inferior bureaucratic positions in the context of their conquest, Indians were obliged to nurse compliance, with its female implications, as a condition of success. In any case, a substantial number of the English felt ill at ease, or thought they ought to, among Indians who demonstrated a notable lack of interest in proving their manhood by overt signs of martial, leather-faced masculinity. They much preferred the "races"—such as the Sikhs and Mohammedans and Rajputs and Pathans—that exhibited a more familiar aggressive spirit.

For a passage that exhibits this particular theme, one may turn to John Strachey's book *India,* a standard training assignment for Indian Civil Service probationers just before the turn of the century. Describing the diverse races of India, it begins with a quote from Macaulay characterizing the Bengalis:

> The physical organization of the Bengali is feeble even to effeminacy. He lives in a constant vapor bath. His pursuits are sedentary, his limbs delicate, his movements languid. During many ages he has been trampled upon by men of bolder and more hardy breeds. . . . His mind bears a singular analogy to his

[5] Percival Spear's *The Nabobs* (London, 1932), pp. 198–99, lists twenty-six quotations expressing European sentiments about Indians in the eighteenth century. Of these, ten include such allusion to weakness or feminine qualities as the following: "Indians are a very sober people and effeminate . . ." (Sieur Luillier, *A Voyage to the East Indies* [1702], p. 285), or the more perceptive, "Tis a mistake to conclude that the natives of Hindustan want courage. . . . With respect to passive courage the inhabitants of these countries are perhaps possessed of a much larger share of it than those of our own" (Major Rennell, Diary, Home Miscellaneous Series, No. 765, p. 182 [20 January 1768]). A. L. Basham has pointed out in *The Wonder That Was India* (London, 1954), p. 172, that homosexuality was rare in ancient India and certainly never became as widespread or legitimate as in Greece or Rome. What precisely the nature of contemporary behavior is would have to be a matter of inquiry, but it is rarely mentioned in nineteenth- or twentieth-century accounts. Morris Carstairs suggests that it occurred in his village among children, was perhaps practiced on occasion among adults, and played a role in phantasy (*The Twice Born: A Study of a Community of High-Caste Hindus* [London, 1957], p. 167).

body. It is weak even to helplessness for purposes of manly resistance; but its suppleness and tact move the children of sterner
climates to admiration not unmingled with contempt. . . .[6]

Strachey himself proceeded to distinguish the more vigorous Mohammedans from the feeble (Hindu) Bengalis, only to be drawn
back in a kind of horrified fascination to his previous subject:

> The Mohammedan peasantry of the eastern portion of the prov-
> ince are men of far robuster character. . . . It has often been said,
> and it is probably true, that Bengal is the only country in the
> world where you can find a great population among whom
> personal cowardice is looked upon as in no way disgraceful.
> This is no invention of their enemies: the Bengalis have them-
> selves no shame or scruple in declaring it to be a fact. . . . This
> for such reasons that Englishmen who know Bengal, and the
> extraordinary effeminacy of its people, find it difficult to treat
> seriously many of the political declamations in which English-
> speaking Bengalis are often fond of indulging.[7]

The contrast to the supple, vapor-bathed creatures was to be found
among the "martial" races, the Sikhs, Pathans, Rajputs, and Muslims, peoples who either by caste ethic, religion, or geographic cir-
cumstance adhered to a more overtly aggressive world view.

The distinction between the martial and non-martial was no in-
vention of the English. It had accumulated ethical and historical
meaning in Hindu caste structure and culture, which inculcated a
non-violent perspective in some castes and an aggressive one in
others. But in English minds at the end of the century, the distinction was stressed as much for its instrumental utility in the imperialist theory as for its academic interest as a description of caste or
regional character. The "martial" races for the most part adhered
to the British raj, not because they were martial—the unlikely collab-
oration of the Pathans with Gandhi must have come as a fearful
shock to many Britons—but for political considerations, the Rajputs
because they were the princes of states whose autonomy was threat-

[6] John Strachey, *India, Its Administration and Progress* (London, 1888), pp.
411–12.

[7] *Ibid.*, pp. 412–13.

ened by a self-governed India, the Muslims because they feared a Hindu majority in an independent India.

Those described as the non-martial races produced nationalism. The allegedly non-violent Brahmans, Vaishyas, and Kayasths provided the shock troops of the pen, office, and pocketbook to publicize, organize, and finance the message of national freedom and regeneration. They launched nationalist polemics in dailies and pamphlets and provided the speakers in official and unofficial public forums to attack government with the Mill and Mazzini inculcated in Anglicized university classes. The Indians whom Englishmen most frequently encountered, once they had established themselves on the subcontinent and the memory of armed resistance had faded, were those recruited to fill bureaucratic roles. By virtue of their tasks, they represented a deceptively one-sided picture of the traditions of the castes from which they were drawn. Beyond this, Englishmen seem to have excluded from their conscious and articulated perceptions evidence conducing to a different picture. Bengali Kayasths have been local notables with fighting traditions as predators and protectors as well as bureaucrats for Moghul and British rulers.[8] Other Bengali castes who served the British also possessed differentiated traditions. But because the imperial capital, Calcutta, was in Bengal it was not unnatural for many secretariat-centered Britons to form their impressions about Indians on the basis of their relations with some Bengalis, generalizing from their civil servants to castes as a whole, and from their regional impressions to India. Such obvious anomalies as, for example, applying non-martial epithets to nationalist Chitpavan Brahmans who spoke for a Maharashtra that had given Britain much pain on the field of battle were easily and often overlooked.

The masculine-feminine distinction overlapped those between "natural" leader and "unnatural" *babu* and between the "real" Indian and the assimilated Indian. What could be more "natural" in a leadership position than a sturdy Rajput whose fighting arm maintained his dominion over the land won by his forefathers and who stood in paternal and autocratic relationship to traditional followers?

[8] For the traditions of the Bengali Kayasthas, see Ronald Inden, "The Kayasthas of Bengal: A Social History of Four Castes" (Ph.D. thesis, Department of History, University of Chicago, 1967).

What less "natural" than the socially mobile men seeking to add political power to traditional priestly, commercial, and literary power, the non-martial Brahmans, Vaishyas, and Kayasths whose new status was often a product of English-created opportunities and who claimed they could lead a parochial and traditional rural India in which they had no long inherited leadership ties? These *nouveau arrivé* politicians and thinkers were not even "real" Indians. They had cut themselves off from India by successfully embracing Western, or more particularly English, ideas and manners. Britons greeted their success in doing so with the special brutality reserved by established classes for new men: if they failed to emulate, they showed their incapacity to appreciate and strive for higher ideals; if they emulated badly, they were easy targets for ridicule; and if they successfully modeled themselves on their masters, they lost their integrity by trying to be something they "really" were not.

What is most significant about these distinctions, and what makes them relevant to the consideration of Gandhi, is that nationalist Indians half-accepted them. No ideology legitimizing superior-inferior relations is worth its salt unless it wins at least a grudging assent in the minds of the dominated. By this measure the unsystematic theory of imperialism was a notable success. Within twenty years of the deliberate exclusion of United Province Brahmans from the Bengal Army because of their leading role in the rebellion of 1857, the idea that Brahmans lacked fighting qualities had become prevailing opinion. Reading recent history back into an undifferentiated past, Indians came to believe that they lacked valor and moral worth. As the young Gandhi put it, "It must be at the outset admitted that the Hindus as a rule are notoriously weak."[9] Why inferiority in arms, technology, and organization, circumstances related to particular historical contexts that may be reversed, has led colonial peoples to more essentialist conclusions about themselves is not entirely clear. The fact that they frequently did come to such conclusions was one of the most degrading consequences of colonialism. This state of mind—a sense of impotence combined with the fear of moral unworthiness arising from impotence—was not unique to India. It provided a central theme in other nationalist movements

[9] *The Vegetarian,* February 28, 1891, in *The Collected Works of Mahatma Gandhi* (Delhi, 1958——), I, 30.

and led to attempts—to use the Chinese nationalist phrase—at self-strengthening.

The Indian fear that their weakness was innate was fed by the scientism of late nineteenth-century post-Darwinian race theory. Ethnologists, particularly ethnologists of India, were fond of imputing a biological fixity to culturally transmitted traits. Further, men of the nationalist generation were by no means sure that they were "natural" leaders or that they were still Indians. A good bit of the Hindu fundamentalism that suddenly gripped men like Sri Aurobindo, raised in an emphatic Western tradition, may be related to this quest to be "really" Indian.

One of the first items on the agenda of nationalism once it stepped beyond the loyal, reasonable, but ineffectual parliamentarism of the early nationalists and began to grapple with the moral and emotional issues of Indian self-definition was the creation of an answer to the charge of national impotence. A variety of answers were formulated —among them the calisthenic muscle-building and aggressive Hindu spirit-building launched by the gymnastic societies of militant Brahmans at Poona, and Dayanand's Arya Samaj path. "Our young men must be strong," Swami Vivekananda urged a generation. "Religion will come afterwards. . . . You will be nearer to Heaven through football than through the study of the Gita."[10] There was the ascetic soldiery of the novel *Ananda Math,* training in a forest Ashram, brave, celibate, sturdy, disciplined, which provided a model for future Hindu fundamentalist parties and the blood deeds of a terrorist generation in Bengal and the Punjab.

There seems to be some perverse historical dialectic in violent Bengali nationalism, as though the young men of Calcutta were saying no to Macaulay's and Strachey's assertions of their physical ineffectualness. But their noes failed to convince. Britain could in good conscience manage young men who threw bombs, especially if they threw them at ladies on a Sunday afternoon. Violence did not in fact turn out to be an effective basis for rallying a mass Indian nationalism. These proofs of courage helped, but they did not help most people, and they did not suffice in the long run to build a sense

[10] Swami Vivekananda, "Lectures from Colombo to Almora," in *The Complete Works of Swami Vivekananda* (3d ed.; Almora, 1922), III, 242.

of national self-esteem. Gandhi's formulation proved a better statement of the issue of courage, and spoke to the issues of potency and integrity as well, even if it did not speak to or for the entire country. Large sections of opinion in Bengal, Punjab, and Maharashtra continued to subscribe to violent methods. Some classes, like middleclass Muslims or non-Brahmans in Madras and elsewhere found his style or his followers too Hindu or Sanskritic; some intellectuals found his religious style and symbolism repugnant to their secular and rationalist values. Still others rejected civil disobedience in the name of establishmentarian or reformist loyalism. Yet Gandhi's approach succeeded in capturing control of nationalist ideology.

Two issues of self-esteem that afflicted Indian nationalism, strength and weakness and cultural integrity, "afflicted" Gandhi in his own life. He confronted them over a period of some thirty-five years before they were fully mastered; his "solution" helped the generations who knew him to deal with them as well. For him the issues of courage and integrity were connected, and he resolved them together. Much of his early life was spent deciding whether he could best master himself and his environment by embracing in greater or lesser measure a British life path or by committing himself to a certain kind of Indian way. The dilemmas of the young Gandhi did in many ways approximate those of the surrounding generations. They can be found in his autobiography, a document that makes clear that Gandhi meant to be simultaneously judged as a private and a public person.

The book he called *The Story of My Experiments with Truth* poses a puzzle for his Western readers. They think they are to read the autobiography of a political leader. Instead they find something so heavily concerned with the Mahatma's "private" activities that it might better have been entitled "Confessions." Confessions are acceptable in saints, like Augustine, or in professional sensualists, like De Sade, or understandable in a tortured exhibitionist, like Rousseau. But in a political man? The relative privacy and reserve of Nehru's autobiography seem more appropriate, not merely as a matter of taste, but as a matter of the life emphasis suitable for a public man. The Western reader is apt to conclude that *My Experiments with Truth* are evidence that the saintly man mattered more than the politician and that Gandhi cared more for his private virtue than his public efforts. But that conclusion rests on the belief, quite pervasive in Western estimates of Gandhi, that saintly striving and political effectiveness must conflict, cannot be merged, and that anyone who seeks to do both must be a fraud either in his pretensions to be a politician or in his pretensions to be a saintly man.

My Experiments with Truth may provide evidence to support different conclusions.[11] In the Indian context it is very much a *political* document, central to Gandhi's political concerns in a double sense, the function it served for him and that which it served for his public. It is from his "experiments in the spiritual field" that he believed he had "derived such power as I possess for working in the political field."[12] And it was not only he who believed this. Many of his immediate and distant followers attributed his political effectiveness to his personal virtue. When thousands assembled to hear him in remote, rural areas, they did so because he was preceded by his reputation for saintliness. When he wrote the autobiography as weekly instalments for his Gujarati journal *Navajivan,* with translations in his English journal *Young India,* he gave wider currency to his attempts at self-perfection.[13] The Gujarati original sold nearly fifty thousand copies by 1940, and the English twenty-six thousand by 1948, making it a best seller in the context of India's literacy and income levels.[14] The installments provided reassurance that the conditions of his political strength had been long preparing and severely tested, even while they conveyed moral aphorisms to young men who would be virtuous. The autobiography, then, must be read with

[11] Erik H. Erikson has suggested the ways in which the autobiography acts not merely as a recollection of the past but as a cautionary tale meant to advise and guide young men, "for the purpose of recreating oneself in the image of one's own method; and . . . to make that image convincing" ("Gandhi's Autobiography: The Leader as a Child," *American Scholar,* XXXV (Autumn, 1966), 636).

[12] *Gandhi's Autobiography, or, The Story of My Experiments with Truth,* trans. from the Gujarati by Mahadev Desai (Washington, D.C., 1948), p. 4.

[13] *Ibid.,* p. 3.

[14] This is in addition to the eight thousand copies the *Navajivan* and *Young India* serializations were selling when Gandhi wrote the autobiography (*ibid.,* pp. ii, iii, and 581).

a particularly sensitive ear, one that hears what he has to say concerning his diet, or his relations to his wife, and considers what it might mean for his political style and for how that style was received. To relegate these remarks to the category of personal frills and curiosities that constitute the gossip rather than the serious significance of a great man is to miss what was central to his leadership.

The small princely state of Porbandar, in Kathiawad, where he was born in 1869, lies on the Arabian Sea, in the center of an area that has always been open to the trade of Persia, Arabia, and Africa, on the one hand, and the interior of India, on the other. He was born a Vaishya, a member of the Modh Baniya caste, one of many trading castes that have flourished in that region because of the hospitable conditions for commerce. His grandfather, whose memory had taken on mythical grandeur for the family by the time Gandhi was a child, served, as members of Vaishya castes often did in western India and the Rajput states, as prime minister of a princely state.[15] Gandhi's father did the same, though with less distinction.

Gujarat resembled the "burned-over" district of western New York in its religious eclecticism and susceptibility to intense religious experience and leadership; it is from its soil that both Swami Dayanand and Mahatma Gandhi sprang. Strains of Hindu, Jain, and Muslim belief found expression in a variety of sects that sought to transcend the clash of faiths through synthesis or syncretism.[16] The religious culture of Gandhi's family reflected many of these ideological forces and syncretic tendencies. Followers of Vaishnavism, a bhakti (devotional) path, they nevertheless adhered strictly to the social and ritual requirements of Brahmanic Hinduism. Jain ideas and practice powerfully influenced Gandhi, too, particularly through his mother: ascetism in religious and secular life; the importance of vows for religious merit and worldly discipline; and *syadvad,* the doctrine that all views of truth are partial, a doctrine that lies at the root of *satyagraha.* Putliba (Gandhi's mother) descended from the Pranami, or Satpranami, sect, whose eighteenth-century founder, Prannath,

---

[15] Prabhudas Gandhi, *My Childhood with Gandhi* (Ahmedabad, 1957), Chap. 2.

[16] Pyarelal [Nair], *Mahatma Gandhi: The Early Phase* (Ahmedabad, 1965), I, 173.

attempted to unify Islam and Hinduism in a Supreme God. Gandhi remembers, in his only visit to the sect's temple, the absence of images and the Koranic-like writing on the walls. Followers of Prannath were forbidden addictive drugs, tobacco, wine, meat, and extramarital relations.[17]

Of the many strands in Gujarat's eclectic and often competing religious cultures, the most powerful in shaping Gandhi's outlook and style was bhakti, the devotional path to religious experience and salvation. "The culture of Kathiawar," Pyarelal writes, "is saturated with the Krishna legend."[18] Ota Bapa, Gandhi's grandfather, was a follower of the Vallabhacharya sect of Vaishnavism whose Krishna-Bhakti doctrine of love of and surrender to God, personified by Lord Krishna, makes Him accessible to all regardless of social standing or cultural background. Both he and Gandhi's father habitually read *Tulasi Ramayana,* a text that became Gandhi's favorite too.[19] It told of Rama's love for his devotees, his graciousness, his compassion for the humble, and his care for the poor. These qualities of bhakti have enabled it to appeal to democratic constituencies and to become the carrier of implicit social criticism of the hierarchy, social distance, and exclusivity of Brahmanic Hinduism.[20] Its contempt for classical Hindu social categories was expressed in the low caste social background of many of those attracted to it, both leaders and followers, and in the substance of bhakti songs, its main means of communication. If bhakti, like chiliastic Christianity but unlike Gandhi's political strategy and methods, sublimated social discontent rather than channeling it in a rebellious or revolutionary direction, the mature Gandhi yet found in the bhakti tradition an orientation and a style that suited him and those to whom he spoke.

Gandhi's mother painstakingly observed the more rigorous demands of her faith. Her strong ascetic demands on herself—"self-

---

[17] *Ibid.,* p. 214.   [18] *Ibid.,* p. 117.

[19] Gandhi's grandfather Uttamchand was a follower of Khaki Bapa, of the order of Ramanand, a bhakta devoted to Rama; both Uttamchand and Gandhi's father, Kaba Gandhi, devoted their later years to reading the *Ramayana* (*ibid.,* I, 179).

[20] The opposition between the bhakti cults and Brahmanic Hinduism is modified by the fact that orthodoxy, too, accepted bhakti as a path to God. See especially the *Bhagavad-Gita.*

suffering," as Gandhi was to call it when he made it part of his political method—seem to have been a central virtue in the Gandhi home. Mrs. Gandhi fasted frequently and practiced other austerities. "During the four months of *chaturmas* Putliba lived on one meal a day and fasted on every alternate day."[21] The concern for non-violence also received impetus from her: Jain monks, with their emphasis on the sanctity of all life, frequented the house.[22]

"Self-suffering" was important in other ways to the family. If one member of the household was angry with another, he would punish him by imposing some penalty on himself. Thus young Gandhi, angry because his family failed to summon to dinner a friend whom Gandhi wished to invite—it may have been a Muslim friend, with whom the family could not dine without transgressing the caste ethic—ceased to eat mangoes for the season, though they were his favorite fruit. The family was duly distressed.[23] On another occasion, Gandhi, finding difficulty in confessing a minor theft to his father, wrote him a note. "In this note not only did I confess my guilt, but I asked adequate punishment for it, and closed with a request to him not to punish himself for my offense."[24] It was the father's self-suffering, not punishment, that he claims to have feared most, although it is possible that he may in fact have feared being beaten. Gandhi's father, in turn, had used the threat of self-punishment in his relations with the ruler he served by announcing he would go without food and drink until arrangements were made for his transport out of the state when his master was reluctant to accept his resignation.[25] And above all, self-suffering in the sense of self-sacrifice was a dominant theme in the life of a boy who, for some three years, daily spent most of his after school hours nursing a sick father—a theme to which we shall return.

[21] D. G. Tendulkar, *Mahatma: Life of Mohandas Karamchand Gandhi* (Bombay, 1951——), I, 28.

[22] Pyarelal, *Mahatma Gandhi: The Early Phase*, I, 214.

[23] Tendulkar, *Mahatma*, I, 31.

[24] *Gandhi's Autobiography*, p. 41. Gandhi's sister Raliatbehn, on the other hand, recalls that Gandhi was quite nervous about the prospect of a beating for this offense (P. Gandhi, *My Childhood with Gandhi*, p. 22).

[25] P. Gandhi, *My Childhood with Gandhi*, p. 22.

Gandhi pictures himself as a shy, fearful, and pathetic child. "I was a coward. I used to be haunted by the fear of thieves, ghosts and serpents. I did not dare stir out of doors at night. Darkness was a terror to me."[26] He feared school and his schoolfellows: "I used to be very shy and avoided all company. My books and my lessons were my sole companions. To be at school at the stroke of the hour and to run back home as soon as school closed—that was my daily habit. I literally ran back, because I could not bear to talk to anybody. I was even afraid lest anyone should poke fun at me."[27] He shunned the actively virile and competitive sports, possibly, as we will presently see, because he was obliged to shun them. He participated in neither cricket nor gymnastics, which a headmaster made compulsory in line with English public school models. Gandhi's father, entertaining a rather different idea of what was good for the character of a young man, had him exempted from sports so the boy might come home and nurse him.[28] It was uncompetitive, unassertive walking that the young man learned to like, and gardening.[29]

His wife Kasturba, who he married at the age of thirteen, was no help in enhancing the self-esteem of a fearful child. She was wilful and self-assertive, did not reciprocate his passion, and resolutely refused to be the deferential Hindu wife he had hoped for, adding to his sense that he could not command where others had traditionally done so.[30] His self-description pictures him as a boy of

[26] *Gandhi's Autobiography*, p. 33.

[27] *Ibid.*, p. 15. Gandhi's relations with his age companions may have been affected by the fact that he would not fall in with the usual rough and tumble of youthful life. He could not be relied upon to tell white lies to cover up group pranks and would not strike back in any encounter. Whatever moral precocity was involved in these deviations received some positive recognition by his schoolmates, who used him regularly as a referee in games. These recollections spring from Gandhi's sister's memories (P. Gandhi, *My Childhood with Gandhi*, pp. 27–28). The memories are retrospective, recalled after Gandhi became "Mahatma," and may deserve a little caution.

[28] *Gandhi's Autobiography*, p. 28.

[29] Pyarelal, *Mahatma Gandhi: The Early Phase*, I, 197.

[30] "She could not go anywhere without my permission . . . and Kasturbai was not the girl to brook any such thing. She made it a point to go out whenever and wherever she liked. More restraint on my part resulted in more liberty being taken by her . . ." (*ibid.*, p. 22).

thirteen or fourteen who had failed to develop a sense of personal competence.

The Mahatma's description of the boy he was probably over-stresses his timid nature. All accounts of his youth speak of his enormous energy, as well as his considerable independence.[31] He was the favored child of both mother and father.[32] Capable of a self-confident naughtiness, he ran away from those sent to find him, scattered the utensils of the home shrine, including the image of the deity, scrawled on the floor, and committed other spirited pranks.[33]

Yet to judge from his subsequent actions one must conclude that he found inadequate support in his immediate environment for solving the issue of personal competence. He felt himself insufficiently strong and courageous and longed to be brave and masterful. The caste ethic of the Modh Baniyas as well as the family's faith closed many paths of assertive self-expression that might seem obvious to a boy beginning to become a man. Sexual expression, although formally sanctioned in marriage, was frowned upon. What one might call culinary masculinity, the eating of meat, was equally discouraged in a society that was vegetarian. The caste ethic, to say nothing of the local Jain influence stressing absolute non-violence, de-emphasized physical aggressiveness, which was in any case against young Mohandas' nature.[34] Not that Gandhi's environment provided no opportunities for self-assertion. The merchant castes of west India have found sufficient scope for assertiveness, even aggressiveness, within the bounds of commercial or bureaucratic caste roles. Members of Gandhi's family, despite the rhetoric of non-violence, allowed them-

[31] "The first three children of Kaba Kaka and Putliba gave them little trouble, but young Mohan was a bit of a problem. Not that he was mischievous or one to annoy his elders. He was not a difficult child but he was exceedingly active and energetic. He was never at one place for long. As soon as he was able to walk about, it became difficult to keep track of him" (P. Gandhi, *My Childhood with Gandhi*, p. 25).

[32] "I was my mother's pet child, first because I was the smallest of her children . . ." (Gandhi as cited by Pyarelal, *Mahatma Gandhi: The Early Phase*, I, 193). Kaba Gandhi believed Mohandas would take his place: "Manu will be the pride of our family; he will bring lustre to my name" (*ibid.*, I, 202).

[33] *Ibid.*, p. 195.

[34] Young Mohandas did not like to fight or hit back (*ibid.*, p. 195).

selves aggressive behavior, including his mother's willingness to see her boys defend themselves and Kaba Gandhi's willingness to beat an offender. But what the opportunities were is less important than how they appeared to Mohandas; he thought himself restricted.

Gandhi staged a massive revolt against his family, caste, and religious ethic in an effort to gain a more helpful perspective. Between the ages of thirteen and sixteen, he undertook a resolute program of transgressing every article of the codes that mattered to those around him. The counselor in revolt was Sheikh Mehtab, a Muslim, significantly enough, representing an ethic quite different from his own, the ethic of one of the "martial races." The friendship was the most significant and enduring of Gandhi's youth, lasting well into his South African years. He sent Mehtab money from England[35] and brought him to South Africa. Mehtab came to live with him there until Gandhi, discovering his friend was bringing home prostitutes, threw him out.[36]

It is usual among Gandhi biographers to endorse the Mahatma's description of the relationship, that he took up Mehtab in order to reform him.[37] It is true in that Gandhi all his life tried to overcome men like Mehtab by "reforming" them. But there was more to the relationship. On the evidence of Gandhi's own words, Mehtab was a model, and a model from whom he only gradually liberated himself. Mehtab was everything Gandhi was not—strong, athletic, self-confident, lusty, bold. As Gandhi writes, he was "hardier, physically stronger, and more daring. . . . He could run long distances and extraordinarily fast. He was an adept in high and long jumping. He could put up with any amount of corporeal punishment. He would often display his exploits to me and, as one is always dazzled when he sees in others the qualities he lacks himself, I was dazzled. . . ."[38]

Mehtab encouraged Gandhi to eat meat, saying that it would have a physiological effect in lending him new strength. "You know how hardy I am, and how great a runner too. It is because I am a meat-eater."[39] But there was a larger social context to the meat-eating

[35] Ibid., p. 211.

[36] Louis Fischer, The Life of Mahatma Gandhi (London, 1951), p. 75.

[37] Gandhi's Autobiography, p. 31.

[38] Ibid., pp. 32–33.   [39] Ibid., p. 32.

issue. It had become attached to the problem of cultural virility for people other than Gandhi. Many people in Kathiawad, according to Gandhi, thought meat-eating was, so to speak, responsible for British imperialism, being the essence that made the Englishman strong. "Behold the mighty Englishman; He rules the Indian small; Because being a meat eater; He is five cubits tall . . ." went the ditty of Gandhi's school days. "I wished to be strong and daring and wanted my countrymen also to be such, so that we might defeat the English and make India free."[40] Actually, Gandhi did not have to look to British culture to discover that meat-eating "produced" courage. The fighting castes of India, particularly the Kshatriyas, have always eaten meat, and it has always been thought to contribute to their strength. But meat-eating was not the only kind of demonstration of strength in which Mehtab supported Gandhi. There was also a brothel episode, presumably meant to lead Gandhi to a more zestful lustiness than the guilty pleasures of his legitimate bed. But Gandhi suffered a Holden Caulfieldesque experience of tentative approach and horrified retreat.[41]

This rebellion was a search for courage and competence, an attempt to overcome fearfulness and shyness through following an ethic other than the one to which Gandhi had been born, an ethic practiced by Englishmen and the "martial races." But it should be pointed out that the search for courage itself exacted a courage of another kind that the ultimately dependent Mehtab did not have. To revolt in secret against strongly held family prejudices over a period of three years required considerable inner strength, strength of the kind the mature Gandhi would have approved, though in the service of other objectives.[42] He demonstrated the same kind of courage, although he described himself as still a coward, when at the age of nineteen, after his father's death, he decided to go to England for an education. He was obliged to confront the opposition of the caste council at Bombay. In an open meeting where he appears to have been afflicted by little of the shyness he always attributed to himself, he faced the elders who forbade his English trip and who

[40] *Ibid.*, p. 34. [41] *Ibid.*, p. 37.

[42] "The opposition to and abhorrence of meat-eating that existed in Gujarat among the Jains and Vaishnavas were to be seen nowhere else in India or outside in such strength" (*ibid.*, p. 34).

threatened all the sanctions of outcasting if he defied their verdict. "I am helpless," he told them.[43]

In some respects, the English experience, during which Gandhi studied for the matriculation exam and was eventually admitted to the bar, represented an attempt to solve the issue of competence and self-esteem by acquiring a new cultural style and by escaping cultural ties that he still deemed in some way responsible for his incompetence and weakness. For three months after his arrival, he dedicated himself to a systematic effort to become an English gentleman, ordering clothing of the correct cut and a top hat in the Army and Navy Stores and evening clothes in Bond Street, worrying about his unruly hair, which defied the civilizing brush, acquiring from his brother a gold double watch chain, spending time before the mirror in the morning tying his cravat, and taking dancing lessons so that he might be fit for elegant social intercourse and violin lessons to cultivate an ear for Western music so that he might hear the rhythm that escaped him when dancing. In the hope of overcoming his incapacity to communicate effectively, he took elocution lessons only to find that they helped him in neither public nor private speaking.[44]

Some of this systematic attempt to approximate urbane English manners stuck for a long time: the pictures of the young Gandhi, as a sixty-thousand-dollar-a-year lawyer in the South Africa of 1900[45]—one is apt to forget that he was capable of that kind of

[43] *Ibid.*, p. 58. The account that he gave to an interviewer from *The Vegetarian,* June 20, 1891, is slightly different. There he says he told the senior patel, who told him crossing the waters was against caste rules: ". . . If our brethren can go as far as Aden, why could not I go to England?" (*The Collected Works of Mahatma Gandhi,* I, 59).

[44] *Gandhi's Autobiography,* pp. 70–71. Gandhi in London "was wearing a high silk top hat burnished bright, a Gladstonian collar, stiff and starched; a rather flashy tie displaying almost all the colors of the rainbow under which there was a fine striped silk shirt. He wore as his outer clothes a morning coat, a double breasted vest, and dark striped trousers to match. And not only patent leather boots but spats over them. He carried leather gloves and a silver mounted stick, but wore no spectacles. He was, to use the contemporary slang, a nut, a masher, a blood, a student more interested in fashion and frivolity than in his studies" (quoted in B. R. Nanda, *Mahatma Gandhi: A Biography* [London, 1958], p. 28).

[45] Fischer, in *The Life of Mahatma Gandhi,* says Gandhi earned five to six thousand pounds a year (p. 74).

worldly success—which present a punctilious late-Edwardian appearance, bear witness to the experience. So did his English, which, after three years in South Africa, bore the marks of relatively cool English understatement. The writings of his early maturity strike quite a different note from the un-English moralizing of the autobiography, written after he had become the Mahatma and had returned to more Indian modes in all respects.[46] His family's clothing and the accouterments of his house were Anglicized on his return to India. Less superficial aspects of English culture left a permanent mark. Throughout his life he remained a barrister, deeply influenced by ideas imbedded within British law, administration, and political values, including respect for correct procedure, evidence, and rights, and for the distinctions and conflicts between private and public obligations.

But the attempts at Anglicization failed to satisfy Gandhi, partly because he could not make a go of it, partly because it didn't "feel" right to him when he could. Besides, the England he met was not the England of public schools and playing fields, of clubs and sporting society, but an England closer to Kathiawad, an England of vegetarian Evangelicals and Theosophical reformers, an England suffering like Kathiawad from the effects of industrialization and protesting against them.[47] After three months he "gave up" much of the Anglicization effort, although less than he suggests in the autobiography, and began a very gradual return to a personal style of life more in keeping with the ascetic, self-denying, and non-violent ethic that he had left behind when he began his rebellion at home almost seven years before.

He started to live very thriftily, partly through economic necessity, partly because the change "harmonized my inward and outward life."[48] Earlier, he had restricted himself to vegetarian restaurants because of a vow to his mother but had remained committed to meat-eating in the interest of reforming the Indian character.[49] Now he

---

[46] See, for example, "The Grievances of the British Indians in South Africa—The Green Pamphlet," written in 1896, in *The Collected Works of Mahatma Gandhi,* II, 1–53.

[47] Chandra Devanesan, *The Making of the Mahatma* (Madras, 1969).

[48] *Gandhi's Autobiography,* p. 75.   [49] *Ibid.,* p. 67.

embraced vegetarianism by choice, in a spirit that stressed a different kind of strength than that promised by meat. He began to rejoice in the effort of denying himself, in the strength of mastering his pleasures. He walked rather than rode to his studies[50] and took up moral and philosophic writings seriously for the first time, although more in the spirit of one seeking confirmation than of one seeking. He was moved by the biblical exhortation "that ye resist not evil" and by passages urging self-suffering as a mode of conversion. Carlyle's hero impressed him as much by his austere living as by his bravery and greatness. He noted passages in the Gita condemning the senses and concluded "that renunciation was the highest form of religion."[51]

In this time lay the beginnings—it took another two decades to complete the process—of a rejection of any solutions to his personal dilemmas that were radically foreign to his early experiences in the Gujarat cultural setting of family, caste, and religion. Solutions drawn from England or from features of Indian culture closer to English culture began to recede. In this period lay the beginning, too, of his construction of an Indian definition for himself, a definition expressed in the Gandhi who in 1906 began political action in South Africa and in 1920 took charge of the Indian nationalist movement. In the long run, these new experiments lead to the development of a personal style consistent with a traditional Indian model rather than with the model of a London-touched barrister, which other Indian nationalists found congenial. The early experiments in vegetarian restaurants and the considered return to an un-English asceticism were not unrelated to those later appeals and techniques of agitation that touched traditional Indian sensibilities and perceptions.

By the end of the English experience, Gandhi had begun to learn that the English solution was not the one to resolve those personal dilemmas that had accompanied him to England. The man who returned to India, and spent several years in practice there, felt himself still a failure. "But notwithstanding my study, there was no end to my helplessness and fear."[52] Though he was a barrister-at-law, more highly qualified than a great many of the traditional vakils

[50] *Ibid.*, p. 73.   [51] *Ibid.*, p. 92.   [52] *Ibid.*, p. 105.

who had no such elevated training, he knew little Indian law and could not even master the fundamental skill of the courtroom lawyer—public speaking. In England, he had made several attempts to give public speeches, generally at vegetarian societies. Each time he failed.[53] On one occasion, to encourage himself, he decided to recite the anecdote of Addison, as diffident as Gandhi, who rose on the floor of Commons and tried to open his speech by saying, "I conceive." Three times the unfortunate man tried to open with the same phrase but could get no further. A wag rose and said: "The gentleman conceived thrice but brought forth nothing." Gandhi thought the story amusing; unfortunately, in his recitation of the anecdote he, too, got stuck and had to sit down abruptly.[54]

His first court case in India was a disaster; obliged to cross-examine plaintiff's witness in a petty case, he was unable to bring himself to open his mouth. "My head was reeling and I felt as though the whole court was doing likewise. I could think of no question to ask. The judge must have laughed, and the *vakils* no doubt enjoyed the spectacle."[55] His model in the law had something in common with the bold Sheikh Mehtab: Pherozeshah Mehta, a strong and effective barrister, who dominated the Bombay bar with his vigorous courtroom style. Gandhi had heard that he roared like a lion in court. But the model seemed increasingly out of reach. He retreated from court work altogether to return, more or less defeated, to the backwaters of provincial Kathiawad, where he took up briefing cases for other lawyers, earning a respectable three hundred rupees per month but feeling that he was getting nowhere.[56] Yet a twenty-three-year-old Indian in 1892 who considered himself a failure at three hundred rupees per month had high standards. At twenty-four a personal tiff with the political agent—an Englishman—at Porbandar convinced him that he had no future there.[57] He determined to retreat from the Indian situation. "I wanted somehow to leave India."[58] The flight seems to have come at the lowest moment of his life.

The low point was also the turning point. His first experiences in South Africa, where he went as a barrister for a Muslim firm, persuaded him that the humiliation and oppression of Indians in South

[53] *Ibid.*, p. 83.
[54] *Ibid.*, p. 84.
[55] *Ibid.*, p. 120.
[56] *Ibid.*, p. 123.
[57] *Ibid.*, p. 125.
[58] *Ibid.*, p. 129.

Africa were worse than in India. He was discriminated against on trains and beaten by a white coachman who laughed at his legalistic insistence upon his rights.[59] Discussing his experience with other Indians, he discovered that the South African Indian community had suffered such humiliations for many years, pocketing insults as part of the conditions of trade. The discovery had a curious effect on his outlook. He recognized, rather suddenly it seems from the autobiography, that the skills that he had acquired in recent years, particularly a facile use of English, a familiarity with law codes and legal processes, and a belief that English justice must be enforced, were desperately needed and lacking among the Indian community. The South African Indians consisted of a merchant community and a much larger group of Tamil indentured laborers. Both lacked political consciousness and skills and were ineffectual at dealing with any part of the environment that transcended their economic tasks.[60] In this setting Gandhi, as the only Indian barrister, found himself to be the entire Indian professional middle classes.

Skills that in India had seemed ordinary here seemed extraordinary and enhanced Gandhi's self-estimate with an apocalyptic abruptness. Within three weeks of his arrival in South Africa, the shy boy of twenty-four suddenly called a public meeting of all Indians in Pretoria for the common discussion of their wrongs and oppressions in the Transvaal.[61] With a new-found authority, the man who had been unable to speak in public rose to sum up the problems of the community and propose an agenda for its amelioration. One has the sense that the overwhelming humiliations of the community around him suddenly carried him beyond the self-consciousness of his own failings, in a manner reminiscent of the "cured" stutterer in Nikos Kazantzakis' *The Greek Passion* ("He Who Must Die"). While speaking in court was an exercise that would show whether he measured up to the standard set by famous barristers like Pheroze-

[59] *Ibid.*, pp. 140–41, 143–44.

[60] Gandhi's first South African client told him: "What can we understand in these matters? We can only understand things that affect our trade. . . . We are after all lame men, being unlettered. We generally take in newspapers simply to ascertain the daily market rates, etc. What can we know of legislation? Our eyes and ears are the European attorneys here" (*ibid.*, p. 173).

[61] *Ibid.*, p. 157.

shah Mehta, a performance profoundly disturbing to a precarious ego, this speech had, ostensibly, nothing to do with his own standing. The new context, service, seems to have made it possible for the young man to do what he could not do when his own reputation was at stake. That service could lend him the effectiveness and potency he otherwise lacked must have had much to do with the life path he chose.[62] Away from home and the omnipresent memorials of early failure and performing a new task, he writes, "I acquired some measure of my capacity."

The South African experience helped him recognize that his salvation lay in devoting himself to the problems of those more helpless than he. As he did so, his capacity to act effectively and courageously grew. The techniques that expressed his new sense of competence rallied Indians to refute English charges of cowardice without, however, repairing to the English standard of courage. His style of leadership confounded the English charge that the new Indian middle classes had lost touch with their own people without, however, alienating those classes.

Gandhi and the New Courage

Indian nationalism had tried the paths of loyal constitutionalism and terrorist violence and found them wanting. Gandhi's answer was *satyagraha* ("truth force"), expressed through non-violent but non-constitutional direct action.[1] *Satyagraha* compels adherence to its

[62] A contributing factor in the success of the first speech may have been that Gandhi spoke in Gujarati. His audience consisted mainly of Memon Muslims, and "very few amongst his audience knew English" (Tendulkar, *Mahatma,* I, 46; see also *Gandhi's Autobiography,* p. 158). It is interesting that when Gandhi returned to India in 1896, with three years of South African successes behind him, he failed once again to manage a public speech before a large Bombay audience (*Gandhi's Autobiography,* p. 216).

[1] For a full-length and sympathetic treatment of Gandhi's philosophic and

cause not by mobilizing superior numbers or force but by mobilizing a general recognition of the justice of its cause. Civil disobedience under certain circumstances compels those who rule to confront the choice of enforcing what they themselves may suspect is injustice or altering policy and practice; for Gandhi, *satyagraha* was a means to awaken the best in an opponent. To resist, to retaliate or strike back if beaten, jailed, or killed, was at once to lack courage and to abandon the means to the common realization of justice. *Satyagraha,* Gandhi said, was "the vindication of truth not by infliction of suffering on the opponent but on oneself." Non-violent resistance to injustice is not unique to the East, much less to India, but it had an extraordinary appeal there during the three decades preceding Indian independence in 1947. Neither constitutional petition and protest nor violent acts of resistance and terrorism had been able to command popular support or unite nationalist leaders. *Satyagraha* did both, in part because Gandhi used it in relation to issues—urban labor grievances, rural tax relief, protests against untouchability—that mobilized new groups for nationalism, and in part because it expressed deeply embedded cultural values in an understandable and dramatic form. Central to these values were a definition of courage and a view of conflict resolution.

The prevailing Western definitions of courage, as well as definitions embraced by those Indians Englishmen called "the martial races," have generally stressed masterly aggressiveness, taking as their model the soldier willing and eager to charge with fixed bayonet the numerically superior enemy in a heroic act of self-assertion. The military analogy is merely the most extreme symbolic expression of a whole set of cultural attitudes—an aggressive, "meat-eating," masterful personal style, overt self-expressiveness, self-confident lustiness —that go well beyond military action. The opposite cultural attitude, cultivated by sections of the explicitly and self-consciously non-martial castes and communities of Indian society, draws on self-control rather than self-expression, on self-suffering, and calls for restraint of the impulse to retaliate. It is misleading to see this willingness to suffer as a failure of will or surrender to fatalism, although it

---

tactical contributions, see Joan V. Bondurant, *The Conquest of Violence; Gandhi's Philosophy of Conflict* (Princeton, N.J., 1958).

may have that meaning as well. Self-restraint may be and has been another way of mastering the environment, including the human environment. The Hindu who sat *dharna* (a protest through fasting) at the house of an alleged oppressor, starving himself, was doing the very reverse of submitting. His courage was in some ways like that which Gandhi stressed. Not to retreat, to suffer pain without retaliation, to stay and suffer more in order to master a hostile or stubborn human reality—these expressions captured important elements of what Gandhi asked of India. Such courage relies for its effectiveness on the moral sensibilities, or at least capacity for guilt, of the more powerful perpetrator of injustice, using his conscience to reach and win him. Gandhi turned the moral tables on the English definition of courage by suggesting that aggression was the path to mastery of those without self-control, non-violent resistance the path of those with control.[2]

This kind of courage tends to go with other cultural practices and attitudes—vegetarianism, asceticism—found especially among the non-fighting twice-born castes, Brahmans, Vaishyas, and Kayasths, who provided the core of nationalist leadership.[3] The traditions of

[2] When with an old man's despair Gandhi watched the violence of partition, he questioned whether Indians had ever understood *his* non-violence. "Gandhi then proceeded to say that it was indeed true that many English friends had warned him that the so-called non-violence of India was no more than the passivity of the weak, it was not the non-violence of the stout in heart who disdained to surrender their sense of human unity even in the midst of a conflict of interests but continued their effort to convert the opponent instead of coercing him into submission" (N. K. Bose, *My Days with Gandhi* [Calcutta, 1953], p. 271).

[3] In Bihar, Kayasths, who constituted 1.18 per cent of the population of the state, constituted 54 per cent of the Bihar Pradesh Congress Executive Committee in 1934. Their disproportionate role in Indian nationalism, like that of other non-martial twice-born castes, was in the first instance due to the fact that they were the first to have Western education (see Rameshray Roy, "Congress in Bihar" [Ph.D. thesis, Department of Political Science, University of California, 1965]).

For the nature of Gandhi's appeal to these men, see Rajendra Prasad, *Satyagraha in Champaran* (Madras, 1928), and *At the Feet of Mahatma Gandhi* (New York, 1961). The Madras Congress until the 1940's was mainly Brahman. For the dominance of Congress politics by Brahmans, and especially the effect this had in limiting its appeal, see Eugene Irschick, *Politics and Social Conflict in South India: A Study of Tamil Separation and the non-Brahman Move-*

these castes were not, of course, uniform. The Brahmans of Maharashtra have often supported violent nationalism, as did the merchant castes of Punjab or the Kayasths and Vaidyas of Bengal. Tilak, Lala Lajpat Rai, and Subhas Bose mobilized different potentials in the same social groups, but with less effect. The Gandhian definition was more resonant with their style and capabilities. The more aggressive kind of courage is, of course, no monopoly of the West but has its counterpart in the ethic of certain Indian castes and communities, just as self-suffering courage has its Western equivalents. The Christian injunction to turn the other cheek, which so impressed Gandhi, is a compelling version of self-suffering—although it is perhaps more closely related to the tender ideals of meekness and love than the acerbic one of self-control.

Self-suffering courage is susceptible of two rather different moral emphases, one that is quite as aggressive in spirit, if not in form, as violence, and one without such overtones. As the traditional weapon of the Brahman, whose protest against oppressive rule was often fasting, self-injury, or even suicide, which would draw upon the oppressor the supernatural sanctions of having caused the death of a Brahman, it substituted spiritual violence for physical.[4] As used in many Indian homes, not merely Gandhi's, where family members sometimes expressed protest by abstaining from meals, it may substitute psychological violence for physical. For Gandhi, such *satyagraha* was nothing more than the passive resistance of the weak.[5] *Satyagraha* in his sense was to be purged of these connotations and infused with a positive moral task. Satyagrahis (those who practice

---

ment (Berkeley: University of California Press, 1969). The Praja Mandals, Lok Parishads, and Harijan Sevak Sanghs (Congress-connected political and social service organizations in Rajasthan) were, through the nineteen-forties, dominated by Brahmans, Vaishyas, and Kayasths (see Rudolph and Rudolph, "Rajputana under British Paramountcy: The Failure of Indirect Rule," *Journal of Modern History* XXXVIII (June, 1966).

[4] For a discussion of the moral and psychological subtleties of non-violence, see Joan Bondurant, "Satyagraha versus Duragraha: The Limits of Symbolic Violence," in *Gandhi: His Relevance for Our Times,* ed. G. Ramachandran and T. K. Mahadevan (Bombay, 1964), pp. 67–81.

[5] N. K. Bose, *My Days with Gandhi* (Calcutta, 1953), p. 270.

satyagraha) were to act so as to elicit the better element in an opponent, rather than the worst, as violence would do. Ill will was the enemy of this effort and hence of *satyagraha*. To purge oneself of ill will was a task requiring strengths most men found hard to command. Gandhi demanded no less of himself and his followers, although he was under no illusion that either he or they always, or even usually, succeeded.

But beyond the distinction between English and Indian definitions of courage lie other cultural differences concerning the honorable and "moral" way to manage conflict in general.[6] The belief that conflicts are best resolved through the frank confrontation of alternatives, the clear articulation of opposites, their clash and the victory of one alternative over the other, is embodied, at least in theory, in much of the adversary legal tradition of the West and in its political life. Traditional Indian ideas of conflict management in both politics and law, as we suggest in Part III, tend to stress arbitration, compromise, and the de-emphasis of overt clashes, of victories and defeats. The rhetoric, if not always the practice, of Indian foreign policy, the continued striving to "restore" consensus processes in village affairs, and opposition to the "evil" of partisanship are receding but still significant expressions of these traditional norms. Their desirability is related to the psychological attraction of self-control and harmlessness over aggressive self-assertion.

Resistance to the notion of conflict arises partly from the romance and reality that surround the image of the village in the minds of many Indians. When the council of five, the *panchayat*, spoke as one, it was said to be the voice of God; it gave expression to the consensus of the traditional moral order. If the consensus was often merely a rhetorical one that obscured real divisions, it was nonetheless valued.

[6] For an extended discussion, on which these pages draw, of Indian approaches to conflict management, see Susanne Hoeber Rudolph, "Conflict and Consensus in Indian Politics," *World Politics,* XIII (April, 1961). Hugh Tinker suggests other threads of the conciliation ethic in his article "Magnificent Failure? The Gandhian Ideal in India after Sixteen Years," *International Affairs,* XL (April, 1964), 262–76. Vallabhbhai Patel had yet another interpretation of Gandhi's consensualism: "You can work in harmony with everybody. It does not cost you any effort. Vaniks (merchants) do not mind humbling themselves" (cited in *The Diary of Mahadev Desai,* trans. from the Gujarati and ed. V. G. Desai [Ahmedabad, 1953], I, 53).

The apotheosized village republic, representative, deliberative, and harmonious, rested on the moral basis of *dharma,* of sanctified custom in which rank and distance, privilege and obligation, rights and duties, were acquired at birth and legitimized by religion.

Studies of village government document the resistance to adversary processes.[7] The consensual process, unlike the adversary, assumes that law will be found (not made) and decisions arrived at by some traditionally recruited body, such as the general *panchayat* dealing with village affairs or the caste *panchayat* dealing with the affairs of a single *jati* (subcaste). All who should be heard will be, and discussion will reveal what most, if not all, agree is the proper disposition of the problem. Discussion, according to one village study, continued until a satisfactory consensus could be arrived at or, in the event of a standoff between two powerful elements, until it was obvious that no agreement was possible.[8] In the meeting's ideal form there remains no opposition, for all have been convinced of the wisdom and necessity of the particular decision.[9] Support is determined not by a show of hands but by judging the participants' sense of moral fitness. Evidence, "witness," and deliberation are important in establishing consensus, but without a common and intimate moral universe that legitimized the domination of some and the subjection of others, traditional consensus would be hard to realize.

Partisanship expressed through the adversary process in politics, government, and law proceeds on the quite different assumption that there are a variety of "interested" answers and that the best one will emerge from the conflict of alternatives. The better each side mo-

---

[7] See also Part III of Lloyd I. Rudolph and Susanne Hoeber Rudolph, *The Modernity of Tradition: Political Development in India* (Chicago, 1967), pp. 251–292, for a discussion of a preference for consensus in the law. Ideas about political consensualism as opposed to adversary modes and partisanship have been most strikingly developed in the postindependence period by Jayaprakash Narayan, who argues for a neo-Rousseauist politics in the context of a radical decentralization of life lived in small-scale communities. See especially his "Reconstruction of Indian Polity," in Bimla Prasad (ed.), *Socialism, Sarvodaya and Democracy* (London, 1964). A vigorous critique and defense of the essay may be found in W. H. Morris-Jones, "The Unhappy Utopia: J. P. in Wonderland," *Economic Weekly,* June 25, 1960; and William Carpenter, "Reconstruction of Indian Polity: Defense of J.P.," *Economic Weekly,* February 4, 1961.

[8] Ralph Retzlaff, *Village Government in India* (Bombay, 1962), p. 24.

[9] *Ibid.,* p. 25.

bilizes its arguments and resources and support, the better the victorious solution will be. The psychological quality of adversary relationships is self-interested and contentious; in a legislature, election, or court, one side wins and the other side loses. The relationship between opponents, at a certain level, is meant to be critical and combative, not conciliatory and accommodating; the arm's length relationship is an aspect of the adversary mode. Compromise, although it is often resorted to, is not the overt objective. There is a final accounting, a choosing between alternatives, and disagreement is exposed and emphasized by quantification through a vote.

To many Indians of Gandhi's time and since, establishing a consensus appeared to sustain and foster community solidarity and mutual accommodation, whereas adversary proceedings in politics and law appeared to sacrifice them by legitimizing partial statements of community purpose and interest. But this is too extreme a juxtaposition: to be viable, adversary proceedings must rest upon substantial if sometimes latent community agreement on values and procedure, and the process of consensual agreement often involves latent partiality and coercion. In the Indian village context especially, consensus was frequently acquiescence in the self-interested rule of a "dominant caste."[10] But the matter of appearance is important; many Indians view the "traditional" consensual way as moral and the "modern" adversary way as evil.

The suspicion of overt hostility seems to be as significant for the nation as the village and for the unconscious as the conscious. In his psychoanalytic study of the twice-born castes in a Rajasthan village, Morris Carstairs found two basic and interdependent patterns—one of mistrust and hostility, which destroyed mutual confidence and often erupted into violence, the other of self-restraint, which characteristically depended on a third person to intervene and bring the

[10] The dominance of higher landowning castes and their special role in determining the nature of the "consensus" are well documented. See, for example, M. N. Srinivas' discussion of the numerically and economically superior Okkaligas in "The Social System of a Mysore Village," and Kathleen Gough's discussion of the Tanjore Brahmans in "The Social Structure of a Tanjore Village," both in McKim Marriott (ed.), *Village India* (Chicago, 1955). These two studies make a useful contrast in that Srinivas indicates that economic power and numerical strength are as important as ritual superiority in determining dominant caste status with respect to village affairs.

antagonists back to their senses. Here human conflict was evidently feared because of its propensity to release uncontrollable passions. "When feelings of ill-will did find open expression . . . the utter collapse of self-control [was] all the more remarkable for its contrast with the formality of normal exchanges." The participants "abandoned themselves to anger with a completeness which previously had been familiar to me only in the temper tantrums of young children. I was able to understand for the first time the epidemic of massacre and counter-massacre which had swept over this 'nonviolent' country only a few years ago."[11] The severe emphasis on selfrestraint, on formality and harmlessness, may well be allied to the omnipresent fear of loss of control. In Carstairs' account, it was the peacemaker who restored restraint by intervening "between the disputants, reminding them how wrong it was to give way to anger, urging self-control and compromise." He found the third-party role of mediator to be so regular a feature of conflict in the village that it recurred in dreams. It was considered better to be the "third party" to a dispute than the victor; "in time, the verb *samjhana* (to impart instruction) became recognizable as an element in everyone's experience, providing a counterpoint to the prevailing distrust. The role of moral adviser, counselling moderation and control of one's passions, is one which compels an impulse to obey, and at the same time, a surrender, however temporary, of one's customary suspiciousness."[12]

Gandhi began to embody these cultural themes concerning courage and conflict resolution in techniques of action relevant to his countrymen's problems in South Africa. Concluding his first big case, the one that had called him there, he believed he had found the path to his future work. Not only had the case been settled by arbitration out of court, but Gandhi had persuaded his client to take payment from the loser in instalments so as not to ruin him. Both actions could have been justified on the mundane ground of ordinary legal or business prudence, but Gandhi did not choose to view the settlement in that light: "My joy was boundless. I had learnt the true practice of law. I had learnt to find out the better side of human nature and to enter

[11] Morris Carstairs, *The Twice Born: A Study of a Community of HighCaste Hindus* (London, 1957), p. 46.

[12] *Ibid.*, p. 47.

men's hearts. I realized that the true function of a lawyer was to unite parties driven asunder."[13] The principle of adversary proceedings, that out of the conflict of two parties, each of whom tries to win by scoring off his opponent, justice will emerge, seemed to him a doubtful doctrine. "The counsel on both sides were bound to rake up points of law in support of their own clients,"[14] he complained. Solutions based on compromise seemed better because they rested on mutual confidence rather than institutionalized conflict.

A more mature Gandhi would formulate the approach in terms of *ahimsa,* the doctrine of harmlessness or non-violence translated into opposition to destructive conflict in general, not merely to physical violence. Had Gandhi developed a different, more aggressive personal style, had he been less diffident, bolder in court and public, he might have taken a different view of the issue of courage and the adversary mode and found himself with or at the head of Indians of quite a different sort. As it was, he turned what he once considered a failing in himself, an incapacity for aggressiveness, into a virtue and an effective political technique. His solutions were of a piece with the renewed concern for the harmlessness ethic of his youth and opposed to the path of aggressive self-assertion that he had tried and rejected.

What Gandhi concluded about the law, he applied thereafter to all other situations of conflict, including his struggles in South Africa and in India. The thread of compromise, of avoiding conflict to find areas of agreement that could produce settlement, remained central to his technique, sometimes to the despair of his followers, some of whom wanted to confront the issue and the enemy by taking a clear stand. To this technique, he added the "witness" of self-suffering. A coercive technique and a means of psychic survival in his home, it was reminiscent of the traditional means that the non-martial classes used to cope with opposition and hostility. When Gandhi fasted or his followers suffered themselves to be beaten, he and they demonstrated the courage required for self-control rather than self-assertion. For those who described such behavior as "unmanly," Gandhi reformulated the imputation. Such non-violence expressed not the im-

[13] *Gandhi's Autobiography,* trans. from the Gujarati by Mahadev Desai (Washington, D.C., 1948), p. 168.
[14] *Ibid.,* p. 63.

potence of man but the potency of woman: "Has she not greater intuition, is she not more self-sacrificing, has she not greater powers of endurance, has she not greater courage?"[15] And the courage of non-violence was, moreover, apt. "Self-suffering" touched the conscience of Englishmen as it might not that of some other imperial rulers.

Self-Control and Political Potency

The distinction between "real" and assimilated Indians, like that between the masculine and feminine races, left a psychic wound. Those Indians who became like Englishmen after being educated in Anglicized schools could no longer be respected nor respect themselves—so went the British imputation—because they no longer recognized their Indian birthright. The "real" India of princes and peasants and martial races retained its integrity; the assimilated India of babus did not. How could the babus expect to lead, much less rule, India? The charge was a telling one, especially in the decades before the turn of the century when nationalism and its leaders were strongly influenced by liberal England and its parliamentary life. However "Indian" the private lives of Ranade, Gokhale, Srinivas Iyengar, and Surendranath Banerjee may have been, their public ideas, idiom, and often dress were those of cultivated English gentlemen. Their nationalism and political principles seemed not to speak to those who lacked their rather special intellectual and cultural experiences. It was convenient for Englishmen to characterize those experiences as somehow fraudulent. Their friends the "real" Indians—peasants untouched by middle class intellectuality, traditional ruling classes—were generally indifferent to nationalist appeals and demands for responsible government, exhibiting instead a gratifying satisfaction with an administrative state managed by British civil servants.

[15] M. K. Gandhi, *Woman's Role in Society*, comp. R. K. Prabhu (Ahmedabad, 1959), p. 8.

The leadership of the political generation preceding Gandhi's, Tilak, Sri Aurobindo, Lala Lajpat Rai, and B. C. Pal, searched for a way to master the moral and strategic consequences of the distinction —and division—between "real" and assimilated Indians. The issue was one of identity, of a national self-definition that could renew a sense of Indian distinctiveness while incorporating ideas suitable for a changing world. It was also one of political effectiveness, of reaching wider constituencies and broadening the base of nationalism. Both dimensions of the challenge pointed toward more traditional symbolism. Many of these leaders embraced traditional symbolism, often supporting, in consequence, conservative Hindu practices, exacerbating Hindu-Muslim relations, and countenancing violence.

Gandhi's response was shaped by such recent national experiences as the evocation of a hero (Shivaji) and religious symbolism by Tilak in Maharashtra, the appeal of sentiment in the politics and literature of the anti-partition movement in Bengal, and the reforming zeal with which the Arya Samaj was able to modify Hinduism in the Punjab and Uttar Pradesh. But unlike his predecessors Gandhi leavened traditional symbolism with reformist ideas, tried to find symbols and issues that would avoid Hindu-Muslim confrontations, and pursued a non-violent strategy. Even if he did not fully succeed, he did distinguish himself from his predecessors by infusing these inherited elements with the exceptionally compelling remorseless moral vision of a "religious." Most striking symbolically was his resuscitation on a national plane of the style of a *sanyasin*, the ascetic seeking enlightenment and virtue. As in his reformulation of the issue of courage, he again responded dramatically to a telling British critique; he was a nationalist leader not cut off from his own people by assimilation.

There is no country whose people do not in some way worry about the private morality of their public leaders. Gossip about the highly placed is never merely gossip; to some extent it reflects the assumption that there may be some continuity between a man's personal self-indulgence or self-constraint and his capacity to act disinterestedly in matters of state and the general welfare. But in modern times we have come to assume that the processes of differentiation that characterize our lives and that touch all our affairs have made private morals less relevant for public action. In the United States, it is assumed that if a senator or perhaps even a president pays attention to ladies other than his wife, doing so will not affect his capacity to manage affairs of state—provided he conducts himself with some circumspection and gives no cause for scandal. It is the differentiation of realms of conduct that suggests to us that conduct in one realm need not be affected by conduct in others.

Certain constitutional assumptions also lie behind the belief that private behavior is to a point irrelevant to public, in a public man. The Western political tradition has been disposed to rely upon external rather than internal restraints, on institutional rather than ethical limits, to control those who wield power. The emphasis on institutional limitations—the balancing of branches of government or of class interests or of church and state—is already found in Greek and Roman thought and remains evident even during the more ethically-oriented periods of medieval polity. Institutional limits have not, to be sure, been the exclusive means of restraining the arbitrary exercise of power. Political theorists in the West have emphasized the virtues kings must have and practice and have found in ethical restraints and their acceptance by kings the means to curb arbitrary action. But in the main, there has been a greater emphasis on institutional rather than on ethical means of ensuring that those who rule use their power for good rather than ill.

It is from "experiments in the spiritual field," Gandhi wrote, "that I derived such power as I possess for working in the political field."[1] His belief that private morality had public consequences reflects the emphasis in traditional Hindu thought on ethical as against institutional restraints. Traditional Hindu political thought, the *dharmasastras* and the epics, stressed the importance of inner over external restraints on rulers, relying not upon countervailing institutions but upon ethical commands to guarantee the public spirit of traditional kings. In practice, of course, countervailing institutions did act as irregular restraints.[2]

[1] See p. 197, n. 10.

[2] In Rajputana, the nobility acted as a restraint upon the activities of Maharajas, as did, in lesser ways, the Brahmans. But these restraints were irregular. See Lloyd I. Rudolph and Susanne Hoeber Rudolph, with Mohan Singh, "A Bureaucratic Lineage in Princely India: Elite Formation and Conflict in a Patrimonial System," *Journal of Asian Studies*, XXXIV (May, 1975).

Ethical commands had a private and a public variant. A king was commanded in private life to restrain his lust, control and master his passions, live simply, and rule his subjects justly. The *Manusmriti* declares "that king [is] a just inflicter of punishment, who is truthful, who acts after due consideration, who is wise, and who knows the respective value of virtue, pleasure and wealth."[3] "For a king who is attached to the vices springing from love of pleasure, loses his wealth and his virtue, but he who is given to those arising from anger, loses even his life. Hunting, gambling, sleeping by day, censoriousness, excess with women, drunkenness, an inordinate love for dancing, singing, and music, and useless travel are the tenfold set of vices springing from love of pleasure."[4] The king who overcomes attachment, who reigns with mind serene, who achieves that expunging of self-interest, can judge clearly and fairly the interest of others. (A problematic assumption, to be sure. There is no reason to believe that such virtue may not itself become a vested interest, seeking to propagate itself among subjects who would live more "attached" lives or giving rise to that *hubris* of the disinterested, that their virtue gives them the right to prescribe for others. A prescription may not be loved any better for being imposed by one who has no "interest" except in virtue.) The public variant of the ethic of restraint was the *rajadharma,* the commands that prescribed for kings what they must or must not do in their public function. There was an implicit assumption that a man who mastered himself could be relied upon to follow *rajadharma.*[5]

We are not concerned with whether these ethical hopes ever became operational restraints for most kings in distant or recent Indian history. The reputation of Indian princes in the last two hundred years would lead one to suppose that an ethic of self-restraint was honored as much in the breach as in the realization. A reputation for

[3] Georg Bühler, *The Laws of Manu—Translated with Extracts from Seven Commentaries,* Vol. XXV of *The Sacred Books of the East,* ed. Max Müller (Oxford, 1886), Chap. VII, vs. 26, p. 220.

[4] *Ibid.,* vss. 46 and 47, p. 223.

[5] "A king . . . who is voluptuous, partial, and deceitful will be destroyed, even through the unjust punishment which he inflicts. . . . Punishment cannot be inflicted justly by one . . . addicted to sensual pleasures" (*ibid.,* vss. 27 and 30, p. 220).

a lively libidinal life may even have enhanced the status of princes and nobles by affording commoners a vicarious opportunity to consume and participate in those pleasures that did not usually come their way.

Yet ethical standards that are steadily breached need not lose their meaning. They remain an ideal, and if someone appears who can enact the ideal, he may fall heir to all the pent up hopes that have survived the experience of repeated disillusion; he may, indeed, command the more respect, inspire the more reverence, because the standard has remained unrealized. It is in this light that the public impact of Gandhi's asceticism must be understood. If Gandhi lived his private life in public, it was because both he and those who observed him believed that a man's claim to be just, to command others, to attain wisdom, was proportional to his capacity for self-rule.

Asceticism was thought to have a power-enhancing function, too. The practitioner of *tapasya* ("austerities") accumulated special powers. This belief rests on what might be called a theory of sexual and moral hydrostatics: the classics suggest, and many Hindus believe, that men are endowed with a certain amount of "life force," which, if used up in passionate or lustful or self-seeking endeavors, will no longer be available for other and higher purposes. Freud, too, found the capacity for sublimation proportional to the diversion from more direct expression of libidinal energies. For him, the discontents arising from self-restraint were the prerequisite, the motor force, of civilization.[6] The *Manusmriti* states the same theory very graphically: "But when one among all the organs slips away from control, thereby a man's wisdom slips away from him, even as the water flows through the one open foot of a water-carrier's skin."[7]

The theory is no rarefied philosophic construct but enjoys popular acceptance. Morris Carstairs, in his study of the twice-born castes of a traditional Rajasthan village, and Joseph Elder, in his study of an Uttar Pradesh village, found much preoccupation with this life force.

---

[6] See Sigmund Freud, *Civilization and Its Discontents.* The idea of a sexual hydrostatics is developed in David Riesman, "The Themes of Heroism and Weakness in the Structure of Freud's Thought," in *Individualism Reconsidered* (Glencoe, Ill., 1954). The Freud comparison has a limit: for him, an excess of restraint produced pathology.

[7] Bühler, *The Laws of Manu,* Chap. II, vs. 99, p. 48.

Carstairs' villagers conceptualized it in a prescientific medical theory as a thick viscous fluid stored in the head; a plentiful quantity of it was thought necessary for fitness and strength. It could be preserved by the practice of celibacy and the careful observance of ritual restraints and commandments and was diminished by ritual carelessness and sexual self-expression. It could also be enhanced by the consumption of certain foods. Unworldly devotees, by their austerity, accumulated such substantial quantities of this life force that they were believed to have special powers, believed to be capable, as ordinary men could not hope to be, of compelling the environment.[8]

Gandhi fully accepted the essentials of this theory: "All power," he said, "comes from the preservation and sublimation of the vitality that is responsible for the creation of life. . . . Perfectly controlled thought is itself power of the highest potency and becomes self-acting. . . . Such power is impossible in one who dissipates his energy in any way whatsoever."[9] If he was able to compel the environment, it was because he practiced *brahmacharya,* celibacy and more general self-restraint; if he was unable to do so, it was because of failures in control. "It is my full conviction, that if only I had lived a life of unbroken *brahmacharya* all through, my energy and enthusiasm would have been a thousand fold greater and I should have been able to devote them all to the furtherance of my country's cause as my own."[10]

In the late 1930's, when the nationalist movement was experiencing severe difficulties, Gandhi characteristically looked for the source of trouble not in society and history but in himself. "A Congress leader said to me the other day, . . . 'how is it that in quality, the Congress is not what it used to be in 1920-25? It has deteriorated'. . . ." Special historical forces were part of the answer, but only a part:

[8] Morris Carstairs, *The Twice Born: A Study of a Community of High-Caste Hindus* (London, 1957), p. 86. Conversely, Joseph Elder found that in "Rajpur" all castes shared the view that intercourse deprived a man of some of his soul stuff and thereby shortened his life ("Growing up in Rajpur," chapter of forthcoming book entitled "Industrialism and Hinduism").

[9] Quoted in Pyarelal [Nair], *Mahatma Gandhi: The Last Phase* (Ahmedabad, 1956), I, 573.

[10] M. K. Gandhi, *Self-Restraint v. Self-Indulgence* (Ahmedabad, 1958), p. 56.

". . . There must be power in the word of a *satyagraha* general—not the power that possession of limitless arms gives, but the power that purity of life, strict vigilance and ceaseless application produce. This is impossible without the observance of *brahmacharya* . . . ; *brahmacharya* here does not mean merely physical self-control. It means much more. It means complete control over all the senses. Thus an impure thought is a breach of *brahmacharya,* so is anger." He had not achieved such complete control—a terrible self demand; had he succeeded, the movement, he thought, would not be encountering difficulties. "I have not acquired that control over my thoughts that I need for my researches in non-violence. If my non-violence is to be contagious and infectious, I must acquire greater control over my thoughts. There is perhaps a flaw somewhere which accounts for the apparent failure of leadership adverted to in the opening sentence of this writing."[11]

The ideal of self-restraint has not been confined to Indian public men; it seems to be broadly shared by Hindu Indians even though the intensity with which it is held varies by caste and locality. Its salience is greater among the higher than among the lower castes.[12] Among higher castes, those who share the more self-expressive Kshatriya (warrior-ruler) culture seem less responsive to the ideal of self-restraint than do the Brahmans, Vaishyas, and Kayasths, who formed so conspicuous a part of Gandhi's devoted lieutenants and followers.

Here, as in other areas of Indian life, the ideal asks more of men than most are able to manage. Not only are students, those who have withdrawn from society or those who live as recluses in distant places, asked to observe it, but so, too, to a lesser extent, are married householders. The result is that the ideal is not often fulfilled.[13] The felt disparity between the moral imperative and the capacity to real-

[11] *Harijan,* July 23, 1938, reprinted in *ibid.,* pp. 150–51.

[12] "My general impression was that conjugal intercourse occurred more frequently and was enjoyed more uninhibitedly among the lower castes than the higher castes" (Elder, "Industrialism and Hinduism," p. 218).

[13] Carstairs suggests that the disparity between the ideal and its fulfilment produces "the commonest expression of anxiety neurosis among the Hindu communities of Rajasthan, and perhaps elsewhere as well" (*The Twice Born,* p. 87).

ize it in daily life—a disparity that suggests that Indians are more prone than others to formulate ideals beyond the capacity of ordi nary men, not that they are more erotic—also helps explain the impact of Gandhi's experiments: his achievement of a goal that many Indians recognize but do not realize became a form of vicarious fulfillment of an ego ideal.

The political effectiveness of Gandhian asceticism, then, lay partly in its expression of the traditional view of how rulers are restrained, partly in its coincidence with ideas about how a man's control over his environment might be enhanced, and partly in the fact that it vicariously achieved a personal moral ideal of many Indians. But there is yet another dimension. A great leader's capacity to compel his environment is related to his belief that he can do so. Such self-confidence creates the phenomenon social science calls "charisma." It involves, on the part of him who possesses it, a belief that he can perform, if not precisely superhuman, then at least extraordinary, deeds. Among those who perceive such self-confidence—the army calls it command presence—it produces a faith that he can indeed do what most men cannot.

In a curious way, the psychological chemistry of the relationship between the public man and his constituents is such that—if everything else is reasonably favorable—the belief produces its own justification. In response to such a leader, followers can sometimes mobilize resources within themselves that they do not ordinarily command, thus corroborating the faith that caused them to respond. The psychological logic of this is the reverse of that envisioned by Freud in his writings on leadership and mob psychology: that in a mass response to an apocalyptic call controls break down and libidinal energies are released in actions that express the lowest common moral denominator.[14] Rather, a great leader may mobilize in his followers un-

[14] From Sigmund Freud, "Group Psychology and the Analysis of the Ego." The following quotations are from *General Selections from the Work of Sigmund Freud,* ed. John Rickman (Anchor ed., 1957). "What it [the group] demands of its heroes is strength, or even violence. It wants to be ruled and oppressed and to fear its masters. . . . All their individual inhibitions fall away and all the cruel, brutal, and destructive instincts are stirred." The burden of Freud's argument lies in this direction, although he concedes that "groups are also capable of high achievements in the shape of abnegation, unselfishness, and devotion to an ideal . . ." (p. 173).

suspected strengths and virtues, superego strivings not previously lived up to, which are made active by his moral challenge. The psychology of leadership has tended to neglect this dimension in its pursuit of the causes and consequences of the demagogue and his mass followers. The fear of mass response should not obscure the creative possibilities of charismatic leadership. Gandhi evoked in himself and those who "heard" him responses that transcended the routine of ordinary life, producing extraordinary events and effects on character, which, metaphorically, can be described as "magical."

We are concerned not only with the abstract dimensions of the theory of asceticism but also with how Gandhi came to believe that through its practice he might compel the environment and how the cultural ideal of asceticism came to mean so much to the private man.

It seems fairly evident that Gandhi's extreme fearfulness and self-contempt as a child had much to do with his relations to an ailing father. Gandhi's marriage at the age of thirteen coincided with a stagecoach accident in which his father was seriously injured, never to recover fully.[15] The event itself was sufficiently symbolic and seemed so to the mature Gandhi, suggesting an inauspicious connection between the son's becoming a man and the beginning of the father's decline. Between the ages of thirteen and sixteen, Gandhi spent a substantial part of his free time nursing and ministering to his father's needs. "Every night I massaged his legs and retired only when he asked me to do so or after he had fallen asleep. . . . I would only go out for an evening walk either when he permitted me or when he was feeling well."[16] The father, at least in these years, appears to have discouraged the more venturesome and independent side of his son's activities and favored those of service and nursing, which the young Gandhi shared with his mother. If Gandhi disliked active sports and ran home anxiously after school, the antipathy was

[15] *Gandhi's Autobiography,* trans. from the Gujarati by Mahadev Desai (Washington, D.C., 1948), p. 20. He eventually died of a malignant growth, pp. 43, 44.

[16] *Ibid.;* p. 43; and D. G. Tendulkar, *Mahatma: Life of Mohandas Karamchand Gandhi* (Bombay, 1951———), I, 27–28. Tendulkar says that Gandhi nursed his father for five years, which would carry the ailment back before the stagecoach accident.

probably partly inculcated. ". . . The reason of my dislike for gymnastics was my keen desire to serve as a nurse to my father. As soon as the school closed, I would hurry home and begin serving him. Compulsory exercise came directly in the way. . . ." And in case Gandhi's "keen desire" should ever be overweighed by an interest in sports, "my father wrote himself to the headmaster saying he wanted me at home after school. . . ."[17]

These restrictions on behalf of nursing, which among other things produced in Gandhi a lifelong love of nursing and medical ministrations—we learn to want to do what we have to do—may not have been easy to accept. What physical or temperamental endowments children bring with them seem in Gandhi's case to have been weighted to the energetic side. His older sister described him as a sprightly boy, active and adventuresome, a boy who liked to get away from home and climb trees and lead his own life. He was, says his sister, "a bit of a problem . . . exceedingly active and energetic. He was never at one place for long. As soon as he was able to walk about, it became difficult to keep track of him. . . ."[18] He was not, in short, the sort of boy to whom the home-bound tasks of regularly nursing a sick father are likely to have come easily and naturally.

The mature Gandhi looked back on this experience with a recollection that suggests he took bitter medicine: "When I was younger than you are today," he wrote his son in 1901, "I used to find real enjoyment in looking after my father. I have known no fun or pleasure since I was twelve"—a passage that seems to be saying two things at once.[19] The father was demanding and probably inspired fear and anger. "I did not talk with him much. I was afraid to speak."[20] Gandhi recalls that he found him short-tempered and remembers an occasion when the father responded with forgiveness rather than fury as one of the most striking and surprising of his youth.[21] A sense of unfreedom pervades the mature man's accounts

[17] *Gandhi's Autobiography*, p. 28.

[18] Prabhudas Gandhi, *My Childhood with Gandhi* (Ahmedabad, 1957), p. 25.

[19] *Ibid.*, p. 31.

[20] Pyarelal [Nair], *Mahatma Gandhi: The Early Phase* (Ahmedabad, 1965), I, 202.

[21] *Gandhi's Autobiography*, p. 12, and the incident of the stolen arm bracelet.

of his youth: "When they [the parents] are no more and I have found my freedom . . ."; "all happiness and pleasure should be sacrificed in devoted service to my parents."[22]

That the story of Maharaja Harishchandra, a well-known classic tale acted by a passing traveling troupe, "haunted" Gandhi as a boy may tell something about Gandhi's feeling for the relationship between father and son. He re-enacted it "times without number"; his ideal was "to go through all the ordeals Harishchandra went through." The maharaja's endless misery and suffering, unlikely to speak to the mind and heart of a Western youth, apparently seemed to the young Gandhi a paradigm of existence and a moral guide. "I literally believed in the story of Harishchandra."[23] The story tells of the king's dreadful degradation as he seeks to satisfy the merciless and relentless demands of a saintly Brahman to whom he owes a debt. The Brahman's insistence on payment, that a promise must be honored, is utterly untempered by common sense or charity. To those accustomed to an ethic of consequences related to human capacities, the Brahman's absolute ethic seems incomprehensible. Maharaja Harishchandra is driven from horror to horror in a descent for which Dante might have found words. His kingdom, wealth, wife, and child gone, he is to serve, as a final degradation, as an untouchable menial among fetid corpses in a cremation ground. Harishchandra's submission is total; he laments but accepts his fate. Self-suffering in the name of honoring duty and of pursuing truth, which Gandhi identified with each other, has its reward.[24] The gods themselves come to his side, rewarding his self-control, fortitude, and respect for truth with heaven itself.

The theme of a severe older man who imposes painful demands that must not be resisted recurs in the story of the boy Prahlad,

[22] *Ibid.*, pp. 20, 36.

[23] *Ibid.*, pp. 16–17. The story of Maharaja Harishchandra occurs in many versions. We have drawn on a translation of a Bengali version by Edward C. Dimock in *The Thief of Love* (Chicago, 1963).

[24] " 'Why should not all be truthful like Harishchandra?' was the question I asked myself day and night," Gandhi writes in his autobiography. "To follow truth and go through all the ordeals Harishchandra went through was the one ideal it [the play] inspired in me" (*Gandhi's Autobiography*, p. 17).

whom Gandhi invoked repeatedly as a model of non-violence.[25] Prahlad, who loves God, is commanded by his father to deny him. When Prahlad refuses, the father has him trampled by elephants, and when he survives, he forces him to embrace a red-hot iron pillar. God springs from the pillar to save the boy and slay the father.

The parent who constrained may not have been easy to love or to respect with a full heart. Not only was he short tempered but also "to a certain extent . . . given to carnal pleasures. For he married for the fourth time when he was over forty."[26] This passage from the autobiography seems mild enough until we recollect Gandhi's harsh view of the carnal life and note that Gandhi ignores an important consideration in his father's decision, the fact that he produced no male heir in his previous marriages and was without hope of having one unless he married again.[27] "If you notice any purity in me," he

[25] Tendulkar, *Mahatma*, I, 77, 169; II, 4, 247, 378. The nearest equivalent in the Judaeo-Christian tradition to the virtues of Prahlad and Harishchandra is probably the virtue of Job—but he does not suffer at the hands of humans. We have stressed for the purpose of this account a particular set of relations in the two stories. But the tales speak for the psychology of the *bhakti* (devotional) cults more generally.

[26] *Gandhi's Autobiography*, p. 12.

[27] "The first marriage," Pyarelal writes, "took place when he was fourteen; the second at the age of twenty-five, after the death of his first wife. From his first and second marriages he had two daughters; the third marriage proved issueless, and his wife was stricken with an incurable ailment which made her an invalid for life. Already then fortyish, without male issue or hope of having any, he yielded," according to Pyarelal's version of these events, "to the importunity of his elders and decided to remarry" (*Mahatma Gandhi: The Early Phase*, I, 186). P. Gandhi, a relative, tells us, however, that "the elders in the family in Porbandar have no knowledge of the third marriage" (*My Childhood with Gandhi*, p. 18). Pyarelal, too, in the quotation above, does not make clear what happened to Gandhi's second wife. Gandhi's allegation of carnality rests not only on the fact of four marriages but also on his father's advanced age ("over forty") at the time of the fourth marriage. Here again Gandhi's feelings may have colored his interpretation of the facts. Pyarelal describes Kaba Gandhi as "fortyish" when he married Putliba, Gandhi's mother. Yet when Gandhi was born his father was forty-seven and had had three previous children, two boys and a girl, by Putliba. The second of these children, Raliat, was "Gandhiji's senior by seven years," a fact that suggests that Gandhi's father may have been thirty-eight or nine at the time of the fourth marriage. See Pyarelal, *Mahatma Gandhi: The Early Phase*, I, 186–87, for the details of Kaba Gandhi's marriages and children.

said to a friend in 1932, "I have inherited it from my mother, and not from my father."[28]

Gandhi dealt with the constraint that he felt surrounded him by acceptance and rebellion, exploring both paths more or less simultaneously. He found a guide in his mother's qualities. She, too, sacrificed herself to an invalid requiring much care. It was her suffering and self-suffering and self-control, particularly the last, that he hoped to emulate.[29] But even while he was forcing himself to exhaust the depths of filial devotion, Gandhi set out on the previously discussed secret rebellion under the guidance of Sheikh Mehtab. He appeared for the nursing work and dutifully ministered each day. But he led a double life. In one, he experimented with everything that was forbidden in the other. Gandhi in his inner being and in his "other" life was quite the reverse of the filial model pictured in the autobiography. His venturesomeness and independence survived the parental restraints—in secret and at a high cost to his conscience.

The demands made on Gandhi's filial devotion were not unique. The relationship between this particular Hindu son and his father gives expression to a more general pattern: service to an aging father who remains in charge of a joint family home after his sons have reached maturity and demands at least formal self-effacement of their masculinity and a commitment to devoted service. The pleasure of filial service is real. Like many cultural demands that initially require sacrifice and discipline, it becomes itself a satisfaction. Yet there may be limits to the kind or degree of self-effacement that can be expected. By the side of the satisfactions, and depending perhaps on the degree of devotion demanded, reside the more or less suppressed discontents of the effacement. The demands of the Hindu joint family, especially as they are expressed in the more ascetic sects and castes like Gandhi's, can require "too much" of some sons. The circumstances of his father's illness, Gandhi's great sensitivity to the moral demands of the culture, and his innate vigor seem to have at once heightened the compulsions of filial devotion and the inner resistance to them. The conflict between duty and an insufficiently

[28] *The Diary of Mahadev Desai,* trans. from the Gujarati and ed. V. G. Desai (Ahmedabad, 1953), I, p. 52.

[29] *Gandhi's Autobiography,* pp. 12, 13.

effaced self was exacerbated. That these events occurred during what a nineteenth-century novel would have called "impressionable years" places them centrally in his development.

Gandhi speaks of the circumstances surrounding his father's death as a crisis that revealed to him his shameful moral insufficiency. The crisis represents a crucial turning point in his gradual commitment to asceticism. Its background included a father who commanded the personal ministrations of his son, superseding the claims of the young man's venturesomeness, and a son who had acquired the self-discipline to meet these demands with apparent equanimity and yet who, at great cost to his conscience, launched a secret massive rebellion. The circumstances themselves are quickly related. Gandhi, who had spent the afternoon as usual massaging his ailing and sinking father, left him to join his wife in their bedroom. She was pregnant and hence ritually impure and sexually forbidden. A short time later, he was summoned to his father's room by an uncle to find him dead. If "animal passion had not blinded me, I should have been spared the torture of separation from my father during his last moments." And, "this shame of my carnal desire even at a critical hour of my father's death . . . is a blot I have never been able to efface or forget, and I have always thought that although my devotion to my parents knew no bounds and I would have given up anything for it, yet it was weighed and found unpardonably wanting because my mind was at the same moment in the grip of lust."[30] The child born after these events died.

The event confirmed Gandhi's readiness to believe that his venturesomeness, especially sexually, was in conflict with his duty to nurse and minister. He generalized this belief over time into the view that a life governed by desire conflicts with one governed by duty. Ministering to those who came to depend upon him as a public man was incompatible with anger and passion. His readiness to interpret his father's death in such terms had the weightiest cultural sanction: Those who acted in the grip of lust could not be guided by duty, whereas those who were capable of restraint could. The caste and sect from which Gandhi came perceived the expressive life in ways that could not balance this interpretation by providing a humane or sentimental view of sexuality. For Gandhi as for many others with

[30] *Ibid.*, pp. 45–46.

similar backgrounds, sexuality was virtually an excretory function, not a vehicle for intimacy. If he slept with his wife, it was because he was weak and could not control his impurity, not because the experience provided a context to express their love. The fact that Gandhi's relationship with Kasturba and hers with him was based on duty and habit meant that the experiences of his own marriage could do little to dissuade him of this view. "The husband," Gandhi later wrote, "should avoid privacy with his wife. Little reflection is needed to show that the only possible motive for privacy between husband and wife is the desire for sexual enjoyment."[31] Such a view of sexuality finds support in the culture and circumstances of the traditional arranged marriage and joint family household. Boys and girls were not taught nor did they have opportunities to learn the manners and mores appropriate for relations with those of similar age but opposite sex before their marriage was arranged to a stranger from within the caste fold. Respect for the older members of the joint family obliged the couple to avoid each other in the daytime and to deny if it should exist any overt expressions of the meaningfulness of their relationship. Before and after marriage there were often few opportunities for the creation of affection, understanding, and reciprocity, of the larger human context of sexuality, and thus it had no chance to stand for anything but itself.

His father's death not only spoke to Gandhi of the horrors of sensuality but also reached deeper into the recesses of his being. Its background, the imperfect realization of filial devotion through self-control and the "descent" into self-expression, suggested to him that a culturally impermissible sentiment, lust, had been brought together with a psychologically and culturally impermissible sentiment, anger, and had produced an unthinkable result. "Lust" had "killed"; in some so far unconfronted recess of himself he had "wanted" it to do so.

The circumstances surrounding his father's death moved Gandhi toward celibacy and the consensual mode. Their appeal and morality reach well beyond any particular life into Indian philosophic and historical thought and experience. To become a *brahmachariya,* to become not only a celibate but also one whose self-control extends

---

[31] Gandhi, *Self-Restraint v. Self-Indulgence,* p. 56.

to anger and aggression, was written large there. Such preoccupations "incapacitated" him for a life of self-expression and aggressive self-assertion. That side of him that had experimented with the cultural style suggested by Sheikh Mehtab—meat-eating, sensualism, conflict and partisanship in law and politics, violent nationalism— fell into the shadow. They were the paradigms of the assertiveness from which he had been systematically and authoritatively deterred during the nursing years. Vegetarianism, *brahmacharya,* consensual modes in law and politics, non-violent nationalism, became the channels of venturesomeness and the means to affect and master the environment. They did not raise the spectre of forbidden conduct or the anger and fatal consequence that it "produced." It was among the Indians at Pretoria that Gandhi was able for the first time to speak in public. He could serve them, minister to their needs, ease their suffering, right their wrongs, modes of action that combined venturesomeness with duty.

When the mature Gandhi spoke of self-control, he had in mind not merely the control of the "carnal self," although that was how he often put it. It was hatred and anger as much as sexual self-expression that he sought to pacify and control. Such emotions did not die easily in him. His capacity for fury at his wife and sons, in whom he could not bear to see the human frailties he would not tolerate in himself, remained long into his South African sojourn. It re-emerged to trouble him in his last years. Yet the energy that lay behind fury and his sexual desire was to be transformed into something constructive. A variety of observers commented over many years on the serenity to be found in Gandhi's presence.[32] But accounts of him by close disciples in his ashram suggest a man who gave them anything but peace; his serenity in great moments and in public life seems to have coexisted with great restlessness and testiness over the details of life. The serenity was, we must assume, most painfully constructed in part out of the necessity of mastering its opposite, internal war. Gandhi's techniques of public action in the nation sought to exclude anger. His private horror of private anger remained. Gandhi turned to the Gita, taking from it an ethic that could serve

[32] "One cannot talk to Gandhi or listen to him or even see him from a distance without becoming aware both of the peace that is in him and of the energy he radiates" (Edmond Taylor, *Richer by Asia* [Boston, 1947], p. 412).

his private and public self: to become he "who gives no trouble to the world, to whom the world causes no trouble, who is free from exultation, resentment, fear and vexation."[33] To live it meant peace from the inner strife between filial duty and self-expression and enabled the public man to inspire the confidence and possess the authority that detachment brings.

There have been simpler explanations of Gandhi's serenity. Ritchie Calder, in *Medicine and Man,* writes: "Whenever Mahatma Gandhi was under the stress of the modern world Rauwolfia would restore his philosophic detachment."[34] This explanation seems to have gained a certain currency despite lack of supporting evidence. In view of Gandhi's profound suspicion of all stimulants or tranquilizers (from coffee through opium) because they distracted a moral man from his essential task of self-control[35] and in view of his belief that avoidance of temptation, by withdrawal from society as a wandering ascetic or as a forest recluse, was a less worthy means to gain self-control, such an explanation seems implausible. The same moral considerations that would have deflected him from becoming a eunuch to control his "lust" would have deflected him from using a tranquilizer to produce serenity. At the level of ethics, serenity assumed for Gandhi the nature of a moral transcendence, not merely freedom from a case of nerves, and its moral significance would have been diminished by the employment of a chemical short cut. At the level of psychology, Gandhi valued self-control too highly, and feared its loss too much, to risk it for gains in what he would have regarded a specious serenity, specious because it involved a dulling of perception and the loss of control. The additional difficulty with the allegation is that none of the Gandhi literature provides evidence for it; one suspects that an era unfamiliar with the moral remorse-

[33] Mahadev Desai (trans. and ed.), *The Gita according to Gandhi* (Ahmedabad, 1946), Chap. XII, vs. 15, p. 312.

[34] Calder, *Medicine and Man* (New York, 1958), p. 50. Calder offers no source for the statement.

[35] See his *Drinks, Drugs and Gambling,* ed. Bharatan Kumarappa (Ahmedabad, 1952). He believed smoking stupefied and liked to cite the case of the hero in Tolstoy's *Kreuzer Sonata,* who kills once a cigarette has numbed his feelings (Pyarelal, *Mahatma Gandhi: The Early Phase,* I, 208).

lessness of a "religious" is too readily hospitable to a biochemical explanation.[36]

Gandhi ultimately took the vow of *brahmacharya,* of celibacy, at the age of thirty-seven.[37] His determination to do so was strengthened during the Zulu rebellion, when, as in the earlier Boer War, he undertook nursing service by forming an ambulance corps. "... The work," he wrote, "set me furiously thinking in the direction of self-control," the self-control that so conspicuously failed him when he last nursed his father.[38] The *brahmacharya* vow culminated a gradual but growing commitment to asceticism. It began before Gandhi left for London as a young man of nineteen when he vowed to his mother that he would not touch meat, wine, or women.[39] It continued there with his principled return to vegetarianism and a growing awareness of and concern for ascetic living. His marriage, because it failed to provide a meaningful alternative to asceticism, strengthened rather than deflected him from the life course leading toward self-control. He gave institutional expression to the simple, unadorned life of limited wants in the Phoenix settlement, the utopian colony he established in South Africa and named after the bird who has no mate but renews life by a somewhat different procedure.[40] Those who lived there followed a Benedictine sort of discipline, each man serving according to his aptitude and calling and at the same time pursuing the Ruskinian virtues of dignity in labor and simplicity of wants.[41]

Phoenix and the *brahmacharya* vow were indispensable preconditions for his first great non-violent resistance campaign. "Without Brahmacharya, the Satyagrahi will have no lustre, no inner strength to stand unarmed against the whole world . . . ; his strength will

---

[36] The one bit of evidence that could prove compatible with everything else we know about Gandhi is an account that he, among the many natural remedies he used in the course of his life, especially for constipation, may have incidentally taken rauwolfia. Such evidence would carry this line of explanation no farther than the discovery of paragoric in a family's medicine chest would establish the existence of an opium habit.

[37] *Gandhi's Autobiography,* p. 254.   [38] *Ibid.*   [39] *Ibid.,* p. 56.

[40] A fact that helped recommend the name to him (P. Gandhi, *My Childhood with Gandhi,* p. 37).

[41] *Ibid.,* pp. 45–46.

fail him at the right moment."[42] He assumed that his capacity to compel the environment depended upon the degree of his self-perfection, the degree to which he had purged himself of lust, self-interest, and anger, and he prepared himself by self-imposed discipline. When things went wrong around him, when he felt helpless to shape events, he would conclude invariably that his impotence to do so was the consequence of a lapse into lustfulness or anger. In such moments, he would retreat to fast and observe other austerities, to renew that inner purity that could give him the strength to affect external events.

The relationship between Gandhi's asceticism and his belief that through it he might compel the environment is arrestingly illustrated by a series of events in his last years. He precipitated a scandal by asking at different times, several young women co-workers to share his bed.[43] The incidents tend to evoke either a kind of lascivious *schadenfreude* or a protective silence.[44] More plausible is the view that they were almost desperate attempts by Gandhi to master tragic and overwhelming events by using an extreme version of an old remedy while relying on the reduced resources of an old man. The events coincide with the frightful period between 1946 and 1948, when, in the midst of the partition bloodshed, Gandhi at seventy-seven brought something like peace to Bengal by becoming what Lord Mountbatten called a One Man Boundary Force.[45]

[42] *Harijan,* October 13, 1940, p. 319; cited in Pyarelal [Nair], *Mahatma Gandhi: The Last Phase* (Ahmedabad, 1956), I, 570.

[43] "He did for her everything that a mother usually does for her daughter. He supervised her education, her food, dress, rest, and sleep. For closer supervision and guidance he made her share the same bed with him" (Pyarelal, *Mahatma Gandhi: The Last Phase,* I, 576). "Gandhiji said that it was indeed true that he permitted women workers to use his bed . . ." (N. K. Bose, *My Days with Gandhi* [Calcutta, 1953], p. 134).

[44] Arthur Koestler overstated the case when he wrote that "the Gandhians . . . were so thorough in effacing every trace of the scandal that [Nirmal Kumar] Bose's book is unobtainable in India" (*The Lotus and the Robot* [New York, 1961], p. 150 n.). We obtained it by writing to a well-known Indian bookseller, and so did several colleagues. Pyarelal's book, a standard work that is everywhere available, discusses the matter in detail.

[45] Pyarelal [Nair], *Mahatma Gandhi: The Last Phase* (Ahmedabad, 1958), II, 382.

He began in the Muslim majority area of Noakhali, where Hindus were being slaughtered, and continued in Bihar, where Hindus were doing the same to Muslims. The work was desperately taxing. His walks took him through riot devastated villages, over difficult countryside, and among people who had lost those nearest to them through ghastly brutalities practiced by neighbors on neighbors. Noakhali deeply shook his serenity: "I find that I have not the patience and technique needed in these tragic circumstances; suffering and evil often overwhelm me and I stew in my own juice";[46] and again, "the happenings in Noakhali succeeded in upsetting me; for there are moments when my heart gives way to anxiety and anger."[47] Nirmal Bose, who worked with him in those days, speaks of him as preoccupied with a way to cope with these events—evidently as much the inner events, the wavering of serenity, the rise of anger, as the external events, the bloodshed all around. His capacity to affect the external, he was confident, rested on his capacity to control the internal. Desperate events required desperate remedies. He warned his friends that he was thinking of a bold and original experiment, "whose heat will be great."[48]

He asked Manu Gandhi, his nineteen-year-old grandniece, to share his bed. He appears to have regarded the matter at one and the same time as a test of his "lust control," whether as a man he could withstand temptation, and of his success in creating in himself the feelings and perceptions of a mother, kin to woman, a test that suggests a certain ambiguity of self-definition. "Manu Gandhi, my grandniece, shares the bed with me, strictly as my very blood . . . as part of what might be my last *Yajna* [sacrifice]," he wrote Acharya Kripalani.[49]

---

[46] Bose, *My Days with Gandhi*, p. 96.   [47] *Ibid.*, p. 107.

[48] "Referring to Manu, he said, that he had been telling her how he personally felt that he had reached the end of one chapter in his old life and a new one was about to begin. He was thinking of a bold and original experiment, whose 'heat will be great.' And only those who realize this and were prepared to remain at their posts, should be with him" (*My Days with Gandhi*, p. 116).

[49] Pyarelal, *Mahatma Gandhi: The Last Phase*, I, 581. Kripalani responded that he trusted Gandhi and that he was sure Gandhi had considered the danger that he might "be employing human beings as means rather than as ends in themselves" (p. 582). One of his skeptical friends was reassured by the sight of

Gandhi had always held, in sharp contrast to some more orthodox views, that self-control was worthless if it was achieved by withdrawal from society and thus from temptation. Only self-control in the midst of temptation was worthy. Now he evidently increased temptation to test and thus strengthen himself. His activities were no secret, although many of his warmest adherents wished they were. He discussed the matter in two prayer meetings in February, 1947, telling his audience—Muslims among whom he was working for peace—that his granddaughter (-niece) shared his bed, that the prophet had discounted eunuchs who became such by an operation but welcomed those who became it by prayer.[50] The scandal seems to have made his task in Noakhali more difficult, and a number of his co-workers left him. These events, if anything, confirmed him in his belief that he had to persist. If he did not have the serenity to bear such disapproval, surely he was not yet master of himself. Bose heard him say to a visitor that "the courage which made a man risk public disapproval when he felt he was right was undoubtedly of a superior order. . . . I get impatient and worried when I am confronted with silly arguments. . . . I sometimes flare up in anger. This should not be so. I am afraid I am yet far from the state of *sthita prajna* (self-mastery)."[51]

These events are not characteristic of Gandhi at the height of his powers. Then, his experiments in self-mastery, while often unconventional, remorseless, and directed at the inner environment, were mingled with great common sense concerning their effect on the world around him. And he was often more sensitive to the proper use of human beings. But the logic of these events, even though executed with the declining moral and psychological capacities of an old man, illuminate the ascetic dimension of his character: to control his outer environment he must control the inner, testing it to the utmost limits.

Gandhi and Manu peacefully asleep. It is relevant for the meaning of these events that Gandhi's bedroom was not private and unaccessible but virtually a public room.

[50] Bose, *My Days with Gandhi,* p. 154. Bose, who acted as Gandhi's Bengali translator, chose not to translate these remarks, a procedure that greatly displeased Gandhi.

[51] *Ibid.*, p. 159.

Gandhi's meticulous concern for diet was related to his quest for sexual asceticism. He had a horror of drink because it threatened to undermine self-control. Moderate in his criticism of many things he found objectionable, he was wholly immoderate in his concern to realize temperance: "Drugs and drink are the two arms of the devil with which he strikes his helpless slave into stupefaction and intoxication."[52] This is not an unfamiliar point of view in men who place a high value on self-restraint. What is a little less obvious is the significance of his concern with food. The cultural context of the concern is the close connection classical Hinduism makes between ritual status and what goes on at either end of the alimentary canal. An extremely fastidious management of both input and output marks the practice of the higher castes. It is possible—although we have not been able independently to verify it—that Gandhi's mother carried this general cultural preoccupation with pollution to extraordinary extremes, deploring that she could not be like the honey bee, who converted all input into the purest output.[53] In her case, the preoccupation was associated with chronic constipation, as it was with Gandhi.

In the Indian cultural setting, the human processing of food has implications that go beyond ritual pollution and ritual rank. Food is also violent or non-violent, as Gandhi explicitly recognized in his early, tentative meat-eating experiments. Vegetarianism has a moral as well as a physiological and cultural dimension. Certain food doctrines concern the man of self-restraint.[54] It is generally believed that some foods, "cool" foods, promote a cool disposition, one that is calm, undisturbed, unaggressive, resistant to lust,[55] whereas others

[52] Reprinted from *Harijan*, May 10, 1942, in Gandhi, *Drink, Drugs and Gambling*, p. 130.

[53] Ranjee (Gurdu Singh) Shahani, *Mr. Gandhi* (New York, 1961), p. 5. Shahani offers no citations.

[54] Many texts stress the connection between food and character, notably the Bhagavad-Gita, which associates types of food with levels in the hierarchy of worshippers; see Gandhi's version, *The Gita according to Gandhi,* Chap. XVII, vss. 4–11, pp. 356–57. The categories of "masculine" or "lusty" foods are similar in other cultures: "We Amhara are tough people. We love to eat hot pepper. We love to drink hard alcohol. We don't like smooth foods" (Donald N. Levine, "The Concept of Masculinity in Ethiopian Culture" [paper delivered at the Fourteenth Annual Symposium of the Committee on Human Development]).

[55] Elder, "Industrialism and Hinduism," p. 217; Carstairs, *The Twice Born,* pp. 83, 84.

produce a "hot" disposition, aggressive and lusty. The cool foods are thought to augment that part of life force conducive to saintly power, the hot that part of life force given to lust. "Ghi (clarified butter) gave one a controlled strength, a power of mind and body that could enable one to perform acts bordering on the divine."[56] Although opinion on which foods precisely are hot and cool is not fully consistent, the cool are mainly milk, clarified butter (*ghi*), curds, vegetables, and fruits.[57] Meat and strong spices figure prominently among the hot. The cool list was largely embodied in that developed by Gandhi and his followers in the twenties and also in the menu adopted at Phoenix settlement in South Africa at the beginning of the century.[58] The list of the twenties included sprouted wheat, sprouted gram, coconut, raisins, lemon, milk, fresh fruit, *ghi*, and honey. Gandhi even had doubts about milk, sharing the fear expressed in certain classical Hindu texts that milk is a stimulant.[59]

"Control of the palate," wrote Gandhi, "is the first essential in the observance of the vow (of celibacy)," and "*brahmacharya* needed no effort on my part when I lived on fruits and nuts alone."[60] This apparently unpolitical subject, too, then, had political relevance: what appeared to some as sheer food faddery was understood by many Indians who read or heard about it as an integral part of Gandhi's efforts at self-mastery and an index of his progress.

Gandhi's efforts to control his sexuality, to achieve, as it were, the serenity of neutrality, were reinforced by his very explicit feminine identification. He found his mother a more appealing figure than his father and tried to be like her rather than him.[61] "But the manner in which my *brahmacharya* came to me irresistibly drew me to woman as the mother of man . . . ; every woman at once became sister or daughter to me."[62] His love of nursing was the most prom-

---

[56] Elder, "Industrialism and Hinduism," p. 186.

[57] *Ibid.*, p. 217; Carstairs, *The Twice Born*, p. 84.

[58] P. Gandhi, *My Childhood with Gandhi*, pp. 36, 50.

[59] Reprinted from *Young India*, July 18, 1927, in *Diet and Diet Reform* (Ahmedabad, 1949), p. 13.

[60] *Ibid.*

[61] See *Gandhi's Autobiography*, Chap. 1, "Birth and Parentage."

[62] Bose, *My Days with Gandhi*, p. 199. Bose throughout offers a psychologically sophisticated account, in which he reveals himself as equally a social scientist and a sympathetic friend of Gandhi.

inent aspect of his maternal capacity: he welcomed all opportunities to practice this skill, acting as midwife at the birth of his fourth son, taking care of his wife and babies when they were ill. In his old age, he liked to think of himself as a mother to his grandniece, Manu, the girl who shared his bed as a daughter might her mother's and who had lost a mother. She has written a book entitled *Bapu— My Mother*.[63] He admired, first in his mother, then in women generally, their capacity for self-suffering. The admiration inspired confidence in women co-workers. When he converted self-suffering into a potent political weapon through non-violent resistance, its implication that it would be necessary to suffer violence without retaliation led him immediately to conclude that women would be most apt at it. "Woman is the incarnation of *ahimsa* (non-violence). *Ahimsa* means infinite love, which again means infinite capacity for suffering."[64] (Again, perhaps a curious definition of love.) His belief had enormous consequences for the politicization of Indian women, many of whom took part in public life for the first time during his non-violent resistance campaigns.

Gandhi built a life on rejecting the aggressive, "masculine" aspect of the human potential, accepting instead the peaceful, communitarian, adaptive aspect associated—in the West—with the culture of women.[65] But if, in law, he adopted conciliation rather than the adversary mode or, in politics, he opposed partisanship and praised consensus, he did so to alter the environment, not in order to yield to it. If we stress Gandhi's feminine identification, it is not, as a friend of the rector of Justin remarks, to invite readers to jump over a Freudian moon. Indian culture appears to distribute somewhat differently among men and women those qualities that the West associates with male and female. Effective masculinity seems to be compatible with a broader range of human qualities than many Americans are inclined to accept. "Male" and "female" are not clear and self-evident, much less dichotomous, categories but open to great variations in cultural patterning. To insist that courage or assertive-

[63] Manubehn Gandhi, *Bapu—My Mother* (Ahmedabad, 1955). She reports him as saying to her, "Have I not become your mother? I have been father to many, but only to you I am a mother" (p. 3).

[64] *Harijan*, February 24, 1940.

[65] David Bakan, "Agency and Communion in Human Sexuality," *The Duality of Human Existence* (Chicago, 1966).

ness must be expressed in familiar patterns and idioms is to miss how others may express them. Gandhi's communitarian and peace-seeking ethic and method, "in the manner of women," evoked a broad and deep response in India.[66]

This-Worldly Asceticism and Political Modernization

Many of those who were Gandhi's followers in the nationalist movement accepted his political leadership even while rejecting or not hearing his message of religious commitment and social reform. With each passing generation his image and ideas have declined in public understanding and acceptance. One era's inspiration has become the next era's cliché. Postindependence Indians have little regard for Gandhi's vision of India as a nation with a special "spiritual" vocation and with the will and means to live simply in self-sufficient villages. One hears less and less in political discourse of the Vedas, Upanishads, and Gita or of the public relevance of the quest for union with the eternal. The conception of India as a spiritual nation formulated in the nineteenth and early twentieth century by Dayanand, Vivekananda, Tagore, Aurobindo, and Gandhi himself played a significant part in shaping India's national identity and helping her to make a name and place for herself in the world. With the coming of independence and democratic self-government, new age groups have emerged for whom the nationalist struggle, in which Gandhi played so central a part, has become a history book happening or the memory of old men's youth. Castes and classes have come to power whose cultural backgrounds, political experiences, and moral concerns are less rooted in the Sanskritic tradition and its ideological norms. They pursue goals that are increasingly instrumental. Self-sufficient villages stand in the way of their quest for a release from poverty and dependence. The otherworldly concerns of Gandhian followers detract from the moral and material tasks of economic development and social mobility.

[66] Again it can be argued that these qualities are particularly appealing to the non-violent twice-born castes.

The men of power in India today also have little patience with Gandhi's postindustrial critique of industrial civilization and the alternatives he advocated. Living in an era when industrialized civilization was already well established in the West, Gandhi was of a nation that was just beginning to industrialize. He could still hear and sympathize with the critics of early industrialism, Ruskin, Thoreau, and the European and American utopian socialists, who found that it brutalized men, alienating them from self and society and depriving them of the capacity to govern themselves. Like those who founded utopian colonies, he hoped to revitalize the village community economically and morally, transforming it into a viable and attractive alternative to urban and machine civilization. By freeing men from the dehumanizing tyranny of artificial wants and the production required to satisfy them, the Gandhian village would enable them to live simple, worth-while lives in meaningful communities. These conceptions have influenced postindependence policies, by providing some of the rationale and legitimation for political and economic decentralization.[1] But they are suspect as an unrealistic village romance that fails to appreciate how rapid industrial development can replace poverty with abundance and national weakness with national power. For many among India's intellectual and professional classes, the village is backward and conservative, a place where higher castes and classes dominate lower and new ideas and technology advance at a snail's pace, the place least rather than most likely to provide the inspiration and the means for tomorrow's utopia.

Both at home and abroad Gandhi's philosophy of non-violence has been more sympathetically and broadly received than has his apotheosis of village life. It helped to explain and legitimize, even if it was not the basis of, Nehru's non-aligned foreign policy, and it continues to influence the political tactics of organized political forces. Abroad, its most conspicuous influence has been on the ideas, strategy, and tactics of Martin Luther King in his struggle to win equal rights

[1] Balwantray Mehta, chairman of the team established to consider the possibilities of decentralizing political decision-making, was an old Gandhian worker from Gujarat. The team proposed schemes which served as the pattern for subsequent legislation establishing *panchayati raj* (local political authorities) at the district, development block, and village levels (Government of India, Planning Commission, Committee on Plan Projects, *Report of the Team for the Study of Community Projects and National Extension Service* [New Delhi, 1957]).

and opportunities for American blacks. Yet it, too, has been a casualty of historical events and forces. Gandhi was gunned down by a fundamentalist Hindu who thought he was too soft toward Muslims and Pakistan. Although just prior to his assassination Gandhi had been able to restore sanity and order in parts of Bengal and in Delhi, he had not been able to do so generally; the partition of India released the furies of communal hatred and vengeance, shattering the civilizing controls of respect for non-violence and for public force. In December, 1961, Jawaharlal Nehru took the decision that he had been resisting for fourteen years, to use military force against the Portuguese colonial presence in Goa. In October, 1962, the Chinese penetrated India's Himalayan frontiers, driving India's badly equipped and trained mountain forces to the plains of Assam. In September, 1965, full-scale hostilities broke out between India and Pakistan. These encounters dramatically illustrated the limits of non-violence in international politics, weakened its hold on the Indian public mind, and undermined its place in official ideology. It still is invoked to help justify India's decision not to build nuclear weapons, but the threat of nuclear proliferation in the region and globally puts support for the policy at risk. The last ten years have witnessed the emergence of a vigorous new nationalism; it is more chauvinistic and parochial than that of Nehru, less tolerant and more intemperate than that of Gandhi. It speaks especially to the urbanized young men who have benefitted from expanding if deficient collegiate education. They and others more senior and influential would like India to have more muscle, larger armed forces and nuclear weapons to lick China, Pakistan, or whoever else might be looking for a fight.

On all these counts, spirituality, the self-sufficient village, and non-violence, Gandhi no longer speaks to the needs of the politically active classes of the sixties. For them Gandhi is a virtuous old gentleman, good in his time. His memory is being ritualized and devalued by proliferation of district town statues and stereotyped praise. But there is an aspect of Gandhi's character and work that is relevant to the political modernizer.

Gandhi's greatest contribution to political modernization was the one we have already discussed, helping India to acquire national coherence and identity, to become a nation, by showing Indians a way to courage, self-respect, and political potency. But because these contributions were rooted in the experience of imperial domination and colored by Gandhi's transcendental morality and appeal to traditional ideas, they have become less meaningful to postindependence generations. It is those aspects of Gandhi's leadership that relate to middle-level norms of conduct and to instrumental rather than ideological effectiveness that remain relevant. Obscured by the grand legacies of saintliness and independence, they require analysis and understanding not only because of their continuing significance but also because they were necessary conditions for Gandhi's greatness.

Gandhi's more mundane contributions to political modernization include introducing in the conduct of politics a work ethic and economizing behavior with respect to time and resources, and making India's political structures more rational, democratic, and professional. A man with Gandhi's spiritual concerns might be supposed to show little interest in the more routine tasks of modern politics. Yet far from being incapacitated for mundane political entrepreneurship by his religious heritage, Gandhi drew from it a this-worldly asceticism. His efforts to build effective political organizations were associated with a psychological disposition toward work and efficiency that mobilized like propensities among those whose lives were affected by his example and teaching.

Gandhi approached his public work with the frame of mind of those modernizing men who confront all tasks with the calculation of the metronome and the balance sheet. While Weber and contemporary social psychologists associate industriousness and the economizing of time and resources with achievement drives rooted in "Protestant" character, Gandhi came to them through familial and religious socialization in the Vaishnavite and Jain traditions of Gujarat. His life course does not support Weber's belief that "it could not have occurred to a Hindu to prize the rational transformation of the world in accordance with matter-of-fact considerations and to undertake such transformation as an act of obedience to a divine will."[2] The disposition to work, save, and rationally allocate

---

[2] Max Weber, *The Religion of India: The Sociology of Hinduism and Buddhism,* trans. and ed. H. H. Gerth and D. Martindale (Glencoe, Ill., 1958), p. 326. In his classic but much disputed *The Protestant Ethic and the Spirit of Capitalism,* trans. Talcott Parsons (New York, 1958), he argued that the modernization that flowed from industrial capitalism in the West was rooted

time and resources in order to realize given goals is not necessarily modern. It appears, for example, among religious orders, both East and West, where self-control and asceticism in the service of spiritual ends find expression, as they did for Gandhi, in strict observance of schedules, hard work at physical, intellectual, or spiritual tasks, and the practice of thrift. Traditional merchant castes, too, such as Gandhi's, the Modh Baniyas, exhibit such psychological dispositions and habits. But it is also true that the elevation of these characteristics to universal virtues is particularly associated with the emergence of modern entrepreneurship and scientific technology and the expectations they raised that men could master their material and human environment. In the West, the preaching of these characteristics as virtues and attempts systematically to inculcate them into

---

in Protestant "this-worldly asceticism," the sanctification of the asceticism and acquisitiveness that made for business success. Weber found in Hinduism the mirror image of Protestant Christianity. Despite his awareness and appreciation of elements of Indian culture and society that were conducive to sanctified asceticism and acquisitiveness, he concluded that "it could not have occurred to a Hindu to see the economic success he had attained in his calling as a sign of his salvation" (*The Religion of India,* p. 326). Milton Singer observes that "on *prima facie* grounds one could make a pretty plausible case for the thesis that Hindu metaphysics should produce just those kinds of 'character' and 'character traits' which Weber regarded as necessary for modern industrial society. . . . But I do not think that such a *prima facie* argument is any more conclusive than the opposite argument, which holds that Hindu metaphysics cannot produce a 'capitalist spirit' in a good Hindu" ("Religion and Social Change in India: The Max Weber Thesis, Phase Three," *Economic Development and Cultural Change,* July, 1966, p. 501). See also his important review article of Weber's *The Religion of India,* in *American Anthropologist,* LXIII (February, 1961), and Amar Kumar Singh's very able criticism of the Weber thesis in an Indian context, "Hindu Culture and Economic Development in India," *Conspectus,* III, No. 1 (1967).

David McClelland's *The Achieving Society* (Princeton, N.J., 1961) is probably the leading example of the use of the Weber thesis by social psychologists. He finds that "Hinduism explictly teaches that concern with earthly achievements is a snare and a delusion. . . . It is hard to see how they [Hindu parents] would set high standards of excellence for their son's performance, or show great pleasure over his achievements or displeasure at his failures" (p. 357). McClelland's exemption of Jains and Vaishnavas, who provide some of India's most successful businessmen, is difficult to appreciate since it is not at all clear that their metaphysics, practice, and socialization differ from those of Brahmans in respects critical for McClelland's theory of the need for achievement.

emerging generations through sermons, aphorisms, penny pamphlets, and public education began in the eighteenth century and peaked in the nineteenth.[3]

Much in the petty details of Gandhi's life corresponds to the practice of those eighteenth- and nineteenth-century figures in Britain and America whose lives and teaching popularized the Protestant ethic and applied technology. Pre-eminent among them in America was Benjamin Franklin. In *Poor Richard's Almanac* the inventor, people's philosopher, and statesman offered practical advice to the modernizing and mobile youth of a bustling, ambitious new nation. Some might boggle at the attempt to bracket Franklin and Gandhi, one a herald, the other a critic, of industrial civilization. At certain fundamental points, indeed, the two men undoubtedly were poles apart. Gandhi would not have enjoyed Parisian life, as did Franklin. And Franklin's attitude was highly instrumental toward the practice of virtue. Gandhi would never have congratulated himself, as Franklin did, by saying: "I cannot boast much success in acquiring the reality of [pridelessness] but I had a good deal with regard to the appearance of it."[4] And Gandhi would have been scandalized by a similar Franklinism: "Nothing [is] so likely to make a man's fortune as virtue."[5] For Franklin, a practical man, moderation—in food, drink, and venery—was a virtue. For Gandhi, a religious who refused to separate means and ends, and found the passions a permanent threat, moderation in these areas of life was a shortfall from virtue. Food should be taken like medicine, privately and sparingly, not for pleasure but to sustain life.[6] Celibacy was too serious to be treated

---

[3] See, for example, *Reinhard Bendix, Work and Authority in Industry* (New York, 1956), and Robert Kiefer Webb, *The British Working Class Reader, 1790–1848* (London, 1955).

[4] Leonard Labaree (ed.) *The Autobiography of Benjamin Franklin* (New Haven, Conn., 1964), p. 159.

[5] Charles L. Sanford, *Benjamin Franklin and the American Character* (Boston, 1955), p. 18.

[6] "His diet," Pyarelal writes, "consisted of goat's milk, raisins and fruit and was weighed out and measured with a druggist's exactness and care. The menu for each meal was adjusted carefully according to how the system had responded to the previous meal, the amount of sleep he had or expected to have, and the physical or mental strain already undergone or in prospect"; *Mahatma Gandhi: The Early Phase* (Ahmedabad, 1965), I, 12.

with "moderation." For Franklin, virtue was useful; for Gandhi, it was self-justifying.

These are important differences but they should not be allowed to obscure what the two men held in common; by exploring the points of congruence, Gandhi's contribution to Indian modernity can be better understood. Gandhi and Franklin subjected their environment to rigorous calculations that linked psychic and material expenditures to their returns. And, despite Franklin's contingent view of virtue, they shared a propensity to invest with moral, not merely utilitarian, implications the observance of certain "Protestant" habits. Silence, order, resolution, frugality, industry, cleanliness, and chastity are seven of Franklin's virtues about which Gandhi would have been enthusiastic. However differently they viewed their ultimate fate, neither man proposed to let the control and mastery of his worldly environment escape him.

It is no accident that a large watch was among the few effects Gandhi valued in his lifetime and left behind at his death.[7] Gandhi was extremely meticulous about time, as it was measured by the clock, the more so as he found a good many of those about him indifferent to its compulsions. He employed his watch as a species of tyrant to regulate his own affairs and the lives of those associated with him. Arrivals and departures frequently were crises; Gandhi considered the normal practice of great public figures, to keep their audiences waiting, a transgression. Many were the arrangement committees and colleagues whom he upbraided for failures on this score. Introducing the venerable B. G. Tilak, who was late, to a conference in 1917, Gandhi remarked: "I am not responsible for his being late. We demand *swaraj*. If one does not mind arriving late by three-quarters of an hour at a conference summoned for the purpose, one should not mind if *swaraj* too comes correspondingly late."[8] Once, in his earlier work in 1917 among indigo workers in Bihar, when it became apparent that a decision to move himself and his co-workers

[7] Nirmal Kumar Bose, Gandhi's able—and skeptical—secretary in Bengal in the mid-forties has developed the theme of Gandhi's preoccupation with time and with the watch (in a lecture, South Asia Seminar, University of Chicago, Spring, 1965).

[8] "Speech at Gujarat Political Conference," in *The Collected Works of Mahatma Gandhi* (Delhi, 1958——), XIV, 48.

would not be carried out by the end of the appointed day, he picked up his bedroll at ten o'clock at night and began to move his effects. His associates, for the most part from the upper castes and classes and accustomed to be waited on by servants and to adjust to their inefficiencies, were obliged willy-nilly to move themselves also.[9]

The timetable he blocked out for his first Indian ashram is faithful to his own schedule and recalls a similar affection for orderly schedules in Franklin. Their respective schedules read as follows:[10]

Gandhi			Franklin	
4	A.M.	Rising from bed	5	Rise, wash and address *Powerful*
4:15 to 4:45		Morning prayer	6	*Goodness!* Contrive day's business,
5 to 6:10		Bath, exercise, study	7	and take the resolution of the day; prosecute the present study, and
6:10 to 6:30		Breakfast		breakfast
6:30 to 7		Women's prayer class	8	Work
			9	
7 to 10:30		Body labour, education, and sanitation	10	
			11	
10:45 to 11:15		Dinner	12	Read, or overlook my accounts,
12 to 4:30 P.M.		Body labour, including classes	1	and dine.
			2	Work
4:30 to 5:30		Recreation	3	
5:30 to 6		Supper	4	
6 to 7		Recreation	5	
7 to 7:30		Common worship	6	Put things in their places. Sup-
7:30 to 9		Recreation	7	per. Music or diversion, or
9		Retiring bell	8	conversation. Examination of the
			9	day.
Note: These hours are subject to change whenever necessary			10	Sleep
			11	
			12	
			1	
			2	
			3	
			4	

[9] Rajendra Prasad, "Gandhi in Bihar," in Homer A. Jack (ed.), *The Gandhi Reader* (Bloomington, Ind., 1956), pp. 149–50.

[10] M. K. Gandhi, *Ashram Observances in Action* (Ahmedabad, 1955), pp. 123–24, and Sanford, *Benjamin Franklin and the American Character,* p. 16. Gandhi did, however adjust his schedule when he was on tour or in action politically.

Franklin's timetable differs from Gandhi's mainly in its less picayune calibrations and in allowing more time for dining.

Gandhi took the timetable most seriously: "All members," runs the first rule of the ashram, "whether permanent or otherwise will turn every minute of their time to good account."[11] A few days after Kasturba died in jail in 1944, his morning meal was served at 11:45 rather than at 11:30; those responsible for the meal were lectured: "You know she never sent me food late, even by one minute."[12] Any item included in his schedule was ruthlessly attended to. In late 1946, when Hindu-Muslim disturbances had broken out in Bengal and Gandhi at seventy-seven went to Noakhali district to try to restore peace, he began his day at 2:30 and took up Bengali.[13] Manu Gandhi's diary records: "After taking fruit juice, he began to pore over his Bengali primer. While doing so, he dozed off for about ten minutes. . . . At 7:25 we started on our day's march, reaching . . . at 8:25 A.M. after a full one hour's walk. Immediately upon his arrival there, he again sat down to do his Bengali lession."[14] His secretary Pyarelal reports that, no matter how late the hour or how heavy the pressure of work, the Bengali lesson was never missed.[15] Manu Gandhi's diary entries, precise to the minute, stand witness to the microscopic relentlessness with which the Mahatma imposed on himself and those around him the discipline of calibrated time.

Gandhi's assiduous thrift expressed itself in the smallest and the largest matters. Like Franklin, he went over his accounts daily[16] and would have approved of the entire catalogue of savings aphorisms, from "a penny saved is a penny earned" onward. The ashram rules not only linked cleanliness to thrift but also provided a practical Indian version of the saving-is-earning theme:

> The split twigs used for toothbrushing should be washed well, and collected in a pot. When they dry up, they should be used

---

[11] Gandhi, *Ashram Observances in Action,* p. 147.

[12] Mukulbhai Kalarthi (comp.), *Ba and Bapu* (Ahmedabad, 1962), p. 105.

[13] Pyarelal [Nair], *Mahatma Gandhi: The Last Phase* (2d ed.; Ahmedabad, 1966), I, 118.

[14] February 2, 1947, cited in *ibid.,* p. 44.

[15] *Ibid.,* p. 41.   [16] *Ibid.*

for starting a fire, the idea being that nothing which can be used should be thrown away.[17]

Gandhi wrote hundreds of important communications on the reverse of old letters and memos. When he began the Natal Indian Congress, he self-consciously avoided the waste and ostentation that often accompanied new organizational beginnings in India. Instead of having receipt books and reports printed he ran them off on a cyclostyle machine in his office, "knowing that in public work minor expenses at times absorbed large amounts. . . ." "Such economy," he instructs the readers of his autobiography, "is essential for every organization, and yet I know that it is not always exercised."[18] In his correspondence with the industrialist G. D. Birla, from whom he extracted vast sums to support various nationalist and service enterprises, a good many letters concern themselves with the saving of bank charges on large transfers.[19]

He worried a good deal about accounting for the public funds with which he was entrusted, beginning in a small way in Natal: "People never cared to have receipts for the amounts they paid, but we always insisted on the receipts being given. Every pie was thus clearly accounted for, and I dare say the account books for the year 1894 can be found intact even today."[20] Returning to South Africa in 1896, he reported in detail to the Natal Indian Congress how he had spent the 75 pounds it had sanctioned toward his expenses, including "Barber, 4 annas; Washerman, 8 annas; Pickwick pens, 6 annas; *Pankha* coolie, 2 annas; Theatre, Rs. 4; Servant Lalu, Rs. 10," and so forth.[21]

Gandhi, who tells us in the first sentence of his autobiography that he belongs to the baniya caste and is descended from shopkeepers, and who spent his formative professional years among Gujarati merchants in South Africa, showed a marked flare for acquiring as well

[17] Gandhi, *Ashram Observances in Action*, p. 151.

[18] *Gandhi's Autobiography, or, The Story of My Experiments with Truth,* trans. from the Gujarati by Mahadev Desai (Washington, D.C., 1948), p. 188.

[19] G. D. Birla, *In the Shadow of the Mahatma* (Bombay, 1953), pp. 1–16, 89, 93.

[20] *Gandhi's Autobiography,* p. 188.

[21] Pyarelal, *Mahatma Gandhi: The Early Phase,* I, 730.

as using money. An incident from the early days of the Natal Congress illustrates his persistence, use of strategy, and sense of timing:

> On one occasion during this money raising tour the situation was rather difficult. We expected our host to contribute £6 [one-fourth Gandhi's initial monthly salary], but he refused to give anything more than £3. If we had accepted that amount from him, others would have followed suit, and our collections would have been spoiled. It was a late hour of the night, and we were all hungry. But how could we dine without having first obtained the amount we were bent on getting? All persuasion was useless. The host seemed to be adamant. Other merchants in the town reasoned with him, and we all sat up throughout the night, he as well as we determined not to budge one inch. Most of my co-workers were burning with rage, but they contained themselves. At last, when day was already breaking, the host yielded, paid down £6 and feasted us. This happened at Tongaat, but the repercussion of the incident was felt as far as Stanger on the North Coast and Charlestown in the interior. It also hastened our work of collection.[22]

Again, in 1919, at a critical point in Gandhi's Indian career, he demonstrated that he recognized the importance of mobilizing financial resources and had the will and the skill to do so. Pyarelal tells us that soon after the Jallianwala Bagh massacre a Congress decision to acquire the park for a memorial to those who had fallen required financial support from the businessmen of Amritsar. Swami Shraddhanand, "the saffron-robed Savonarola of Northern India," told the assembled businessmen that "India's glorious past and her lofty ancient cultural tradition" called upon them to rise to the occasion but his "eloquence produced no . . . results." Pandit Mada Mohan Malaviya, founder and chancellor of the Banaras Hindu University and popularly known as "the silver-tongued orator of the Congress," also cajoled the Amritsar business community, by telling its members that if they would only unloosen their purse strings dharma, artha, kama, and moksha, too, would be theirs, but to no avail. "Finally, Gandhi spoke. . . . In level tones he told them that the target had been fixed.

[22] *Gandhi's Autobiography,* p. 187.

It had to be reached. If they failed in their duty he would sell his Ashram and make up the amount. He would not let the sanctity of the national resolve, to which he had been a party—so had they been too—be lightly treated. . . . The required amount [five lakhs of rupees] was subscribed on the spot."[23]

"I must regard my participation in Congress proceedings at Amritsar," Gandhi confesses, "as my real entrance into the Congress politics." His experience there "had shown that there were one or two things for which I had some aptitude." Not only did he succeed in raising the money to acquire Jallianwala Bagh but he was also appointed one of the trustees to raise and administer an additional five lakhs to construct a national memorial there. Pandit Malaviya had had the reputation of being Congress' best fund-raiser "but I knew that I was not far behind him in that respect." It was, Gandhi adds, "in South Africa that I discovered my capacity in this direction." Malaviya had succeeded by turning to India's rajas and maharajas; "but I knew," Gandhi observes, "that there was no question of approaching" them for donation for the memorial. It was under these circumstances that "the main responsibility . . . fell, as I had expected, on my shoulders." Gandhi turned to the business community of Bombay and was again strikingly successful. "The generous citizens of Bombay subscribed most liberally, and the memorial trust has at present a handsome credit balance in the bank."[24]

Gandhi's ascendancy in the Congress was associated not only with his organizational and idiomatic skills and popular touch but also with his financial capacities. More than any other Congress leader, he had access to the purses (as well as the hearts and minds) of India's business communities, an access he used to generate financial support for Congress even while recruiting merchants, traders, and industrialists into organizations and activities associated with nationalism and social reform. While there was no doubt a conservative political dimension to this support, it is difficult to see how, with public patronage and resources in British hands, the professionalization of Congress politics could have been achieved otherwise.

[23] Pyarelal, *Mahatma Gandhi: The Early Phase*, I, 6; *The Collected Works of Mahatma Gandhi*, XVI, 468.

[24] *The Collected Works of Mahatma Gandhi*, XVI, 596–97.

Evidence of Gandhi's industriousness and productivity can be found in his rigid adherence to schedules; the frequency and pace of his interviews; the volume of letters, reports, petitions, and articles that issued from his pen; the number and scope of his tours; and his leadership and management of literary, reform, and spiritual and political organizations and activities. Ordinarily Gandhi maintained his schedule while on tour, doing his daily writing on trains and in way stations. The collected works, which will run to some one hundred volumes, greatly understate the level of his productivity because speeches and statements that did not enter into the public record and letters that were not directed to officials who filed them or to adherents who saved them will not be recorded there. The enormous volume of replies to unknown or obscure inquirers—Nirmal Kumar Bose recalls that in Noakhali he "refreshed" himself with a six-page letter to an unknown young man seeking his advice on marriage arrangements—and a significant volume of public mail are simply lost.[25] In the busy days of the nationalist movement, many who might have kept records found it hard to do so between jail terms; others were not disposed to keep files. But we do know that it took some half-dozen well-trained assistants to help him handle his daily mail and that he took keeping up with it very seriously.

He did a great deal, and he applied exacting standards of accuracy, clarity, and efficiency to all of it. "His energy," Pyarelal tells us, "was phenomenal. . . . One day I actually counted 56 letters which he had written in his own hand." In the midst of din and disorder, his "remarkable faculty of switching on and off his mind to and from anything at will and to remain unaffected by his surroundings" enabled him to carry on with his usual pace and efficiency. "He had a passion for precision and thoroughness in the minutest details . . . and enforced military discipline and clock-work regularity in his own case and expected the same from those around him. . . . He insisted on his desk being always clear and woe to anyone of his staff who referred to him a letter more than forty-eight hours old. . . . Any reply of more than five or ten lines was as a rule consigned to the waste paper basket. The address was no less minutely scrutinized. Not to know . . . the exact location of an out of the way place in India was re-

[25] From a lecture by N. K. Bose, South Asia Seminar, University of Chicago, Spring, 1965.

garded as a culpable failure. Vagueness about train timings or the exact time it took for the post to reach its destination by a particular route was another cardinal sin. . . ."[26] His public reports, petitions and demands reflect the capacity for orderly clear argument and meticulous care for facts that he had developed as a successful lawyer.[27]

Gandhi's this-worldly asceticism took its meaning in the context of larger motives and meanings. Those who practice it cannot know direct rewards but they remain alert for signs of grace. Gandhi associated his reception by the Indian people with the potency of his charisma and saw it as a visible recognition that his worldly asceticism made him worthy. Public influence was the coin in which he measured his worldly success. "The incomparable love that I have received has made it clear to me that they in whom truth and the spirit of service are manifested in their fulness will assuredly sway the hearts of men and so accomplish their chosen task."[28]

But Gandhi was never certain that he was one of those in whom the spirit of truth and service was sufficiently manifest. Some of the energy that he invested in worldly asceticism must have arisen from this uncertainty. It is in his relationship to *darshan* (view of an auspicious object, such as a temple deity, king, or holy man from which the viewer gains merit or good fortune) that these uncertainties become clear. Soon after his return to India in 1915, Gandhi first confronted his *darshan* dilemma—whether his capacity to give and people's eagerness to receive *darshan* was a worldly sign of his spiritual achievements or whether it was an expression of his vanity and their irrationality. At the Kumbha Mela, a vast religious assemblage of pilgrims and sadhus held once every twelve years, *darshan* seekers did not allow him a minute to call his own. It was then, he

[26] Pyarelal, *Mahatma Gandhi: The Early Phase*, I, 12.

[27] See, for various examples, "Extracts from Minutes of Chamaparan Agrarian Enquiry Committee," *The Collected Works of Mahatma Gandhi*, XIII, *passim;* "Letter to the Secretary, Passenger Grievances Committee, Rangoon, July 25, 1917" (with reference to the bad lot of deck passengers of the British India Steam Navigation Service), *ibid.*, pp. 476–78; and "Report of the Commissioners Appointed by the Punjab Sub-Committee of the Indian National Congress" (1920), *ibid.*, XVII, 114–292.

[28] "Punjab Letter," *Navajivan*, November 11, 1919, in *The Collected Works of Mahatma Gandhi*, XVI, 282.

tells us, "that I realized what a deep impression my humble services in South Africa had made throughout the whole of India." And, in almost the same breath: ". . . The *dharsanvalas'* blind love has often made me angry, and . . . sore at heart."[29]

Four years later, as he was establishing his ascendancy in the nationalist movement, Gandhi found, on the one hand, that "the affection that I am receiving from men and women here in Lahore [and throughout the Punjab] puts me to shame," and on the other, that "the unique faith of India and the frankness and generosity of our people enchant me." Not only did "young and old . . . come all day to have *darshan* of [Gandhi]," but also it was impossible for him to go out alone. "I simply cannot check them," he complained. More disturbing was the thought that he knew of nothing in himself that made him "worthy of giving *darshan*"; he found it "intolerable" that they should want *darshan* from a "mere servant." Nor did the people "profit in any way by having *darshan*." "If I keep on giving *darshan*," he commented ominously, "my work will suffer."[30] A month later, in Wazirabad, he had grown tired of *darshan*. ". . . In the end we had to keep the doors closed . . . ; it is not possible simultaneously to work and to give *darshan*."[31]

"No man," he stated flatly, "is great enough to give it." He found that he was embarrassed by the experience and wanted to put a stop to it. But to do so would hurt people's feelings, and he had "not yet found it possible to do this." Perhaps his courage was "inadequate" or his judgment "clouded"; more likely "my principle of non-violence does not allow me to hurt people's feelings." "I do," he protested, ". . . make every effort to extricate myself from this dilemma." But his solution, tentatively stated in 1919 but developed into a habit over the years, was not to choose between *darshan* and work but to try to do both: "At present, even when people come for *darshan*, I continue to write and do other work."[32]

However much Gandhi found himself unworthy of *darshan* and giving it a threat to his work and serenity, he could not escape the

[29] *Gandhi's Autobiography*, p. 475.

[30] "Punjab Letter," *Navajivan*, November 11, 1919, p. 282.

[31] "Punjab Letter," *Navajivan*, December 7, 1919, in *The Collected Works of Mahatma Gandhi*, XVI, p. 325.

[32] "Punjab Letter," *Navajivan*, November 11, 1919, pp. 282–83.

feeling that it expressed in worldly terms some measure of other-worldly approbation, that it was a sign of grace. "Man's instinctive urge to worship," he found "admirable."[33] The test for worship was the worthiness of its object, and Gandhi found it hard to accept that he and those who came to him for *darshan* were engaged in a mutual fraud upon each other. "It is perfectly clear to me that this relationship is the miracle wrought by even a small measure of devotion to truth and service. . . . I am making a prodigious effort to live up to these two principles."[34]

Toward the end of his life, as he was leaving for Noakhali to try to still the communal passions unleashed by partition, the old man in a train was still not certain whether his spiritual virtue and worldly asceticism made him worthy of such attention. But he persisted, mindful of the possibility that he might be and in the belief that effortfulness would make it so:

> The journey proved to be as strenuous as many had feared. There were mammoth crowds at all big stations on the way. At places it was like a swarming ant-heap of humanity as far as the eye could reach. The crowd clambered on the roofs of the carriages, choked the windows, broke glass, smashed shutters and yelled and shouted till one's ears split. They pulled the alarm-chain again and again for *darshan,* making it necessary to disconnect the vacuum brakes. . . . Later in the evening, Gandhiji sat with his fingers thrust in his ears to keep out the shouting when it became unbearable. But when it was proposed to him that the lights be switched off to discourage *darshan* seekers, he turned down the suggestion by saying that the simple faith of the masses demanded that he should serve them with the last ounce of his energy. . . .[35]

Gandhi's version of this-worldly asceticism led him to rationalize and extend the organizational bases of Indian political life. Soon after Gandhi returned to India in 1915 he recognized that Congress could not achieve the goals of national mobilization, social reform, and political freedom as long as it depended exclusively on talking

[33] *Ibid.*, p. 282.   [34] *Ibid.*, p. 283.

[35] Pyarelal, *Mahatma Gandhi: The Last Phase,* I, 4.

shops by, for, and among the English-educated elite. Legislative debates at the center and in the provinces and the formulation of resolutions at Congress annual sessions could not, by themselves, realize these goals. Until opinion was organizationally related to the aspirations and objective needs of popular social and economic forces, it could be neither legitimate nor politically effective. One of Gandhi's most important contributions to political modernization was to help Congress become a mass political organization, manned by full-time political workers and capable of mobilizing public opinion and bringing it to bear on governmental policy and administration. All that has been said and written about Gandhi's shifting the arena and method of Indian politics from persuasion of the government by elites to direct action among the people has obscured a parallel and equally important shift that he inaugurated, building a political organization.

Gandhi began building political organizations well before he entered Indian politics. Visiting India from South Africa in 1901, he was disappointed by what he witnessed at a session of the Indian National Congress. An association of political amateurs in an era that was ready for political professionals, the Congress provided an annual forum for liberal nationalists to address adherents and sympathizers but found it difficult to translate words into action because it lacked the continuity and specialization that permanent structures and full-time personnel make possible. "The Congress," Gandhi observed, "would meet three days every year and then go to sleep. What training could one have out of a three days' show once a year?"[36] He deplored Congress' slovenly procedures and its subordination of efficiency to ceremony. "I also noticed the huge waste of time here. . . . There was little regard for economy of energy. More than one did the work of one, and many an important thing was no one's business at all."[37] Too many people came and too few had the inclination or the means to take the business at hand seriously. "The procedure was far from pleasing to me. . . . There was hardly any difference between visitors and delegates. Everyone raised his hand and all resolutions passed unanimously."[38]

Gandhi had established his first political organization seven years

---

[36] *Gandhi's Autobiography*, p. 274.

[37] *Ibid.*, pp. 278–79.   [38] *Ibid.*, p. 281.

earlier, in 1894.[39] The Natal National Congress was a cadre organization, meticulously organized, that demanded of its members a continuous and high level of commitment. At the end of its first year it had a membership of 228 drawn from the prosperous middle-class section of the South African Indian community.[40] Those who failed to pay their subscription or missed six consecutive meetings were struck off the rolls.[41] The subscription was substantial; at three pounds per year (paid in advance) it represented, for example, 1 per cent of the salary Gandhi received in 1894, a salary that enabled him to maintain the style of life characteristic of the white middle classes.[42] A number of middle-class merchants participated in door-to-door canvassing, a labor that Gandhi evidently considered good experience for testing their commitment.[43] The Congress met monthly to discuss policy and pass on expenditures.[44] Its objectives were not unlike those of the caste associations emerging in India: it published and distributed pamphlets on problems confronting Indians as a subject community facing dominant white South Africans; provided legal assistance to indentured Indians; represented Indian interests in legislative and administrative contexts; and worked to upgrade the manners and life style of the community.[45]

Recognizing that political consciousness and organization without political skills inhibited personal confidence and public effectiveness, Gandhi worked to repair the political skills of Natal Congressmen. "People had no experience of taking part in public discussions. . . . Everyone hesitated to stand up to speak. I explained to them the rules of procedure at meetings. . . . They realized that it was an education

[39] Pyarelal, *Mahatma Gandhi: The Early Phase*, I, 435.

[40] *Ibid.*, p. 489.   [41] *Ibid.*, p. 436.   [42] *Ibid.*, p. 431.

[43] *Gandhi's Autobiography*, p. 186. The group included Messrs. Dawud Muhammed, Moosa, Haji Adam, Mohamed Casam Jeeva, Parsi Rustomji, and Gandhi (Pyarelal, *Mahatma Gandhi: The Early Phase*, I, 437). That Gandhi's early political experiences should have placed him with men who were not intellectuals, who were conservative, merchants, and mainly Muslim, helps explain his later propensity to believe that these groups, in addition to the liberal, Anglicized, intellectual Hindus, could be won over to the nationalist movement.

[44] Pyarelal, *Mahatma Gandhi: The Early Phase*, I, 436.

[45] *Ibid.*, pp. 436, 438.

for them, and many who had never been accustomed to speaking before an audience soon acquired the habit of thinking and speaking publicly. . . ."[46]

The meetings were conducted in Gujarati; if expatriate Gujarati merchants without formal schooling were to participate, there was no other choice.[47] These early experiences contributed to Gandhi's recognition that the use of English inhibited the Indian National Congress and to his optimism concerning the effect the use of regional languages would have on political participation and national consciousness.

Gandhi extended the reach of the Congress by proliferating branches in ten centers outside the territorial jurisdiction of the parent Natal organization.[48] These new structures retained the vanguard qualities of the original organization by being composed of a few, well-placed, committed, and active members.

On his return to India in 1915 he applied the ideas and methods that he had developed in South Africa to the first political organization he joined, the Gujarat Sabha, converting it from an *ad hoc* society that met annually to pass resolutions into a permanent structure whose executive conducted a year-long program of activities.[49] Gandhi was quite explicit about his intention to make politics more professional and to associate it with permanent specialized structures:

> Conferences do not, as a rule, at the end of their deliberations leave behind them an executive body, and even when such a body is appointed, it is, to use the language of the late Mr. Gokhale, composed of men who are amateurs. What we need is men who would make it their business to give effect to the resolutions of such conferences. If such men came forward in great numbers, then and then only will such conferences be a

[46] *Gandhi's Autobiography,* p. 187.

[47] Pyarelal, *Mahatma Gandhi: The Early Phase,* I, 439.

[48] *Ibid.,* p. 442.

[49] N. D. Parikh, *Sardar Vallabhbhai Patel* (Ahmedabad, 1955), p. 43. It is this program that drew Patel, subsequently one of the Congress' great organizational talents and a man impatient with bodies of a deliberative nature only.

credit to the country and produce lasting results. At present there is much waste of energy.[50]

If the professional revolutionary and the professional politician represent two types of the modern political specialist, the Gandhian professional embodies qualities of both without fully resembling either. The professional revolutionary was first given historical expression in the seventeenth century by the "saints" of the English civil war and subsequently elaborated upon by the Jacobin and Bolshevik of the French and Russian revolutions.[51] The professional politician developed out of the experience with competitive democratic politics in western Europe and America.[52] The Gandhian model of politics as a vocation emerged in the years immediately following his return to India in 1915. Although in its particulars this type was related to the Indian cultural context, it has more general application as an example of the professionalization of peaceable ideal politics. Its concern for spiritual meaning, its emphasis on service, its insistence on non-violent means, and its suspicion of power distinguish the Gandhian from the other two models.

Like professional revolutionaries, Gandhian professionals gave the highest priority in their personal lives and public actions to ideologically defined ends, but unlike revolutionaries, they gave equal priority to non-violent means. Modern political specialists, regardless of type, must attend to the requirements of mobilizing and representing particular classes, communities, and interests. For professional politicians, this task tends to become an end in itself since it is the prescribed means for acquiring power. For revolutionaries, mobilization and representation are options to be used under certain historical con-

[50] "Speech at Gujarat Political Conference (Godhra, November 3, 1917)," in *The Collected Works of Mahatma Gandhi,* XIV, 49–50.

[51] See Michael Walzer, "Puritanism as a Revolutionary Ideology," in *Political Theory and Ideology,* ed. Judith Shklar (New York, 1966), p. 64, where he argues that the saints were entrepreneurs, but in politics, not economics. His view of the saints as political specialists is elaborated in *The Revolution of the Saints: A Study in the Origins of Radical Politics* (Cambridge, Mass., 1965).

[52] See Max Weber, *Politics as a Vocation* (Philadelphia, 1965), in which he describes types of professional politicians, particularly the lawyer, journalist, and "demagogue" of the postdemocratic era.

ditions. Gandhians used mobilization and representation as a means to help realize certain ideal goals, such as national freedom or social justice, by making their claims more legitimate and effective. Like revolutionaries but unlike politicians, Gandhians placed self-sacrifice above self-assertion and service to the cause and those whom it was to benefit above considerations of personal popularity or advantage.

Gandhian professionals can also be distinguished from both revolutionaries and politicians by their orientation toward power. Revolutionaries must seek and use power if they are to model a new society; it is good societies that produce good men, and power is a necessary instrument for the realization of good societies. Politicians, too, must seek and use power. In establishing their mandate to govern, to realize certain ideal and material goals, and to allocate resources, patronage, and honor, politicians find the pursuit and deployment of power an integral part of their work. For Gandhians, the desire for power, like any other passion (such as sex or anger) destroyed self-control; without self-control neither serenity nor mastery of the environment nor virtue was possible. By aspiring to power, a man demonstrated his unfitness to exercise it. To seek and use power instrumentally, to put it in the service of worthy ends, was possible, but the danger of attachment to power had to be constantly guarded against. The uses of power were, in any case, limited; the cure for the ills that afflicted state or society lay in changing men's inner environment, their hearts and minds, not their laws and institutions. Virtuous men made for a virtuous society, just as virtuous rulers were the ultimate guarantee of good government.

None of these three modern political specialists can admit that the possession and use of power is an end in itself; their legitimacies depend upon its use in achieving objectives that transcend power. Yet revolutionaries and politicians recognize power as an integral and necessary aspect of their role, whereas Gandhians do not. Gandhi managed the incompatibility between the corruption inherent in seeking power and his insistence that organizational power was a prerequisite for political effectiveness by a contingent and temporary relationship to political and other organizations. His example in building organizations, such as the Natal Congress or the Gujarat Sabha, ashrams, service societies, and the Congress itself, and then leaving them to the direction of others, or disbanding them when he thought their goals had been realized (as he attempted to do with the Congress in 1948 after independence had been achieved), set the standard for the relationship of Gandhian professionals to organizational and political power.

When Gandhi in 1920 was able to bring his organizational ideas to bear on the Indian National Congress, he proceeded to make its structure and procedure more rational, professional, and democratic.[53] The nationalist leaders of each province had been drawn from narrow strata of the English-educated whose connections with popular, "vernacular" structures, opinion, and organized interests were tenuous and haphazard. No one was disturbed by the overrepresentation that followed when the host provinces of Congress annual sessions sent more delegates than those more distant. The Congress, Gandhi objected, placed "no limit to the number of delegates that each province could return."[54] Election to the Subjects Committee, then the Congress' highest executive organ, was not based on any explicit principles of representation or procedure; "there was," Gandhi observed, "hardly any difference between visitors and delegates."[55] Most business was settled beforehand by informal gatherings of Congress notables.[56] Gandhi relates the fate in 1901 of his resolution before the Subjects Committee:

> "So have we done?" said Sir Pherozshah Mehta.
> "No, no, there is still the resolution on South Africa . . . ," cried out Gokhale.
> "Have you seen the resolution?" asked Sir Pherozshah.
> "Of course."
> "Do you like it?"
> "It is quite good."
> "Well, then, let us have it, Gandhi."
> I read it trembling.
> Gokhale supported it.
> "Unanimously passed," cried out everyone.[57]

[53] At the Congress session in December, 1919, Gandhi was asked to revise the constitution of the Congress (*The Collected Works of Mahatma Gandhi*, XVII, 487, n. 2).

[54] *Gandhi's Autobiography*, p. 598.

[55] *Ibid.*, p. 282.

[56] *Ibid.*, p. 596.

[57] *Ibid.*, p. 281.

Even the battles of 1905–6 between moderates and extremists, battles prophetic of those to come over the conflicting claims of alternate strategies, leaders, ideologies, and regions for dominance within the organization, did not elicit efforts to rationalize representation, procedure, and membership.

Gandhi's draft of a new constitution provided for manageable size, defined procedures, and "scientific" representation. "Without that," he wrote, "the Congress will remain an unwieldy body and we would not be able to carry the weight we otherwise could. . . . I have attempted to give the Congress a representative character such as would make its demands irresistible."[58] Although he was obliged to accept six thousand rather than one thousand as the limit on the number of delegates to attend annual sessions, he did succeed in introducing regular procedures for the selection of delegates and the president by creating an orderly, graduated structure of party organizations with fixed jurisdictions, rights, and responsibilities.[59] He also succeeded in establishing rules for the selection of the Subjects Committee and for voting at annual sessions and in converting the informal committee of notables into a new executive organ, the Working Committee.[60]

The structural core of Gandhi's democratization of the Congress lay in the proliferation of units capable of attracting and channelling a mass membership base. The Subjects Committee, Annual Session, Provincial Congress Committees (PCC's), and District Congress Committees (DCC's) were already in existence, but they were geared to a limited membership.[61] Gandhi expected that "the delegates will

[58] Letter from Gandhi to N. C. Kelkar, July 2, 1920, in *The Collected Works of Mahatma Gandhi*, XVIII, 3.

[59] *Gandhi's Autobiography*, p. 613.

[60] The new All-India Congress Committee (AICC) became the Subjects Committee; its procedures were fixed; delegates alone were permitted to vote; and their qualifications had to be ascertained (see articles XXV, XXVI, XII, and XI, respectively, of the Congress Constitution adopted at Nagpur [*The Collected Works of Mahatma Gandhi*, XIX, 190–98]). Article XXIV of the Nagpur Constitution provides for the Working Committee (*ibid.*, p. 197).

[61] Constitution of 1908: Arts. 4, 6–8 (PCC's), 9–12 (DCC's), 24–25 (Subjects Committee), in M. V. Ramana Rao, *Development of the Congress Constitution* (New Delhi, 1958), pp. 13–14.

be elected only through the choice of millions. . . . Every person wishing to join a unit of the Congress is given the right to do so by paying the fee of four annas [about .08 cents in 1920] and signing the Congress creed."[62] The pre-1920 PCC's could not accommodate a mass membership base because their boundaries, which coincided with the administrative boundaries of British India, cut across those of language, with the result that English literacy was virtually a prerequisite for participation. "In so far as Congress is concerned," Gandhi held, "we should re-divide India into provinces on a linguistic basis."[63] His constitution did so, creating twenty-one Provincial Congress Committees each corresponding to a linguistic region. The new PCC's succeeded, although not as much as Gandhi expected they would, in transforming Congress from an elite to a popular organization.[64] Part of the difficulty, then as now, lay in creating structures below the District Congress Committees that could be assigned powers and responsibilities capable of attracting sufficient devotion to insure continuity and effectiveness.[65]

Gandhi also moved to remedy the lack of professional staff and continuous attention to business. "The Congress," he observed, ". . . had practically no machinery functioning during the interval between session and session";[66] "only one of the three general secretaries was a functioning secretary, and even he was not a wholetimer."[67] Gandhi urged that "the secretaries of the Provincial Congress Committees and the District Congress Committees should, so far as possible, be whole-time workers, and may, if necessary, be paid out of the Provincial or District funds."[68] He also provided for the

[62] "Nagpur Congress," *Navajivan,* January, 1, 1921, in *The Collected Works of Mahatma Gandhi,* XIX, 207.

[63] Letter from Gandhi to Chairman, AICC, September 25, 1920, in *ibid.,* XVIII, 289.

[64] "Nagpur Constitution," Article V, in *ibid.,* XIX, 191.

[65] For the party arrangements at the DCC and *taluka* or *tehsil* level (smaller administrative units within a province), see "Draft Model Rules for Provincial Congress Committees," in *ibid.,* XIX, 217–19. The elections to the PCC's and the AICC were to be indirect, DCC's electing PCC's and these electing the AICC (see Nagpur Constitution, Article XIX, in *ibid.,* XIX, 195).

[66] *Gandhi's Autobiography,* p. 597.   [67] *Ibid.*

[68] "Draft Model Rules for Provincial Congress Committees," pp. 218–19.

national and state organs meeting throughout the year; the Working Committee and the All-India Congress Committee (the AICC, which assumed most of the responsibilities of the Subjects Committee) were to meet periodically and the PCC's at least once a month.[69]

Gandhi's reform of Congress in 1920 may not have made it into as popular and representative a political structure as was his intention,[70] but there is no question that he did succeed in changing it from an elite to a mass organization. In doing so he not only changed fundamentally the character of the nationalist struggle for independence but also modernized Indian politics by moving it in a professional and democratic direction and by providing the organizational base, procedures, and habits for national politics.

The Private Origins of Public Obligation

The supersession of private and familial obligations by a public ethic in the conduct of government remains an unfinished item on the agenda of political modernization in India. In the name of such obligations friends and relatives often request public men to use discretion or to bend rules in allocating public resources and places. The dilemma is not peculiar to India; in Britain, too, at an earlier stage of its political development, when bureaucratic norms were struggling for recognition, the principle of "connection" did battle with that of a public ethic. In an era of monarchical and aristocratic politics, a public man's network of relatives, "friends," and dependents expected him to secure places and promotions, favorable rulings, and

---

[69] *Ibid.*, p. 219.

[70] Gopal Krishna points out that the Congress membership in the high recruitment year of 1921 was only 1,945,865 ("The Development of the Indian National Congress as a Mass Organization, 1918–1923," *Journal of Asian Studies*, XXV [May, 1966], 419–20).

contracts for them. In return he expected them to act in his interest.[1] The standards of British public life that haunt many Indian intellectuals and some of her public men today are the product of a later era, ironically enough, the era during which Britain devised more effective and impersonal means for ruling India.[2] It was not, for example, until 1853, when the Indian Civil Service was established, that appointments to places in India formally ceased to be part of the East India Company's patronage, and even under these changed circumstances, it was some time before they ceased to be governed as much by the requirements of (English) private and familial obligations as by those of a public ethic. And while Americans tend to associate patronage and the more general disposition of the "spoils" of pub-

[1] See Part I, sec. I, of Lloyd I. Rudolph and Susanne Hoeber Rudolph, *The Modernity of Tradition: Political Development in India* (Chicago, 1967), nn. 22 and 23.

[2] The conflict between crown and parliament for control of East India Company patronage and spoils was an important component in the growth of responsible government in Britain; see C. H. Philips, *The East India Company, 1784 to 1834* (Manchester, 1940), the standard work on the company's administration and political management. The Northcote-Trevelyan reforms of 1856, which laid the basis for a modern civil service in Britain, arose out of the establishment of the Indian Civil Service three years earlier in clauses 36 and 37 of the India Act of 1853. Sir Charles Trevelyan and Lord Macaulay, both of whom served in India, were the leading spirits in the creation of the ICS, and Trevelyan along with other public figures who had returned from India played important parts in British civil service reform.

The patronage of the East India Company was in the hands of the members of the company's Court of Directors. The twenty-four members of the court shared in the appointments; in making them, they were required to state in an official document the nature of their relationship with the person being appointed and to swear that they had received no money for making the appointment. Between 1809 and 1850, 54.69 per cent gave "friendship" and 23 per cent gave "kinship connections" (B. S. Cohn, "Recruitment and Training of British Civil Servants in India, 1600 to 1800," in *Asian Bureaucratic Systems Emergent from the British Imperial Tradition* ed. Ralph Braibanti [Durham, N.C., 1966], pp. 103–4). The directors, Cohn concludes, "formed a tight society, bound by culture, economic interest, and social relations. . . . It is likely that from 1840 to 1860 fifty or sixty interconnected extended families contributed the vast majority of the civil servants who governed India" (pp. 109, 111), a situation not unlike that prevailing in India where rajas drew their bureaucrats from particular families within one or more caste communities (see Rudolph and Rudolph, "Oligopolistic Competition among State Elites in Princely India," in George Marcus, ed., *Ethnographic Studies of Elites* (Santa Fe, [forthcoming]).

lic office with the establishment of Jacksonian democracy, the practice of aristocratic Britain and of princely India makes clear that honoring private and familial obligations in the allocation of resources and places is by no means confined to democratic regimes.[3]

Whether or not a public or private ethic dominates the conduct of public business reaches beyond the nature of regimes to normative and structural factors that can be shaped by the influence of a great leader. In India, traditional primary-group obligations have been peculiarly compelling. Countervailing obligations to civic virtue or public law, so helpful in the European context in establishing the ascendancy of a public ethic, have found relatively little support in traditional norms and institutions. To establish the idea of public obligations in this setting was a task of considerable proportions. While the norm that Gandhi established has often won rhetorical rather than behavioral adherence, it remains the most significant indigenous statement of civility, paralleling and reinforcing the imported British statement.

The roots of Gandhi's attachment to a public ethic lie in the "first shock" of his adult professional life when he was humiliated by the outcome of an attempt to oblige his brother. The incident brought into conflict two versions of obligation, the one associated with the joint family, the other with norms of bureaucratic impersonality. The incident followed on the heels of Gandhi's failure, upon his return from England in 1891, at the age of twenty-four, to establish himself as a Bombay barrister. He had retreated to Rajkot and the security, dependence, and self-effacement of his eldest brother Lakshmidas' joint family—a position that must not have pleased an independent young man who had been given special advantages as his father's chosen son (to study in England) so that he could lead his family in new directions. The incident's shattering effect on his pride freed him from a course that might have confined him to a far more conventional life; it determined him to leave India for South Africa and strengthened his commitment to public as against familial obligation.

Lakshmidas, head of the Gandhi family after Kaba Gandhi's death in 1886, was suspected by the political agent, E. C. K. Ollivant, of complicity in the unauthorized removal of jewels from the Rajkot

---

[3] *Ibid.*

state treasury. As secretary and adviser to the young prince, Rana Bhavsing, before he inherited the throne, he was thought to have suggested or abetted the removal. At the least, he was charged with having failed to report it, becoming an accessory after the fact.[4] The older brother asked the younger to intervene with the political agent on the strength of a passing acquaintance in England.

The request posed a problem of conduct to which Gandhi was already exceptionally sensitive. His return to Rajkot had been marked not only by a sense of failure but also by an awareness that, by meeting his brother's terms, he had sacrificed his integrity and independence. His brother's firm, consisting of two petty pleaders, Lakshmidas and his partner, gave him work drafting applications and memorials. "For this work I had to thank influence rather than my own ability, for my brother's partner had a settled practice."[5] To get this work, Gandhi confesses, "I had to compromise the principle of giving no commission, which in Bombay I had so scrupulously observed." " 'You see,' " Lakshmidas told Mohandas, " '. . . if you refuse to pay a commission to my partner you are sure to embarrass me . . .' "; since he and Mohandas shared a common household, Lakshmidas continued, they would in any case share their earnings. ". . . To put it bluntly," Gandhi writes in his autobiography, "I deceived myself . . ." in agreeing to abandon the principle of not paying commissions.[6]

Lakshmidas' request exacerbated these doubts:

> My brother thought I should avail myself of the friendship and, putting in a good word on his behalf, try to disabuse the Political Agent of his prejudice. I did not at all like this idea. I should not, I thought, try to take advantage of a trifling acquaintance in England. If my brother was really at fault, what use was my recommendation? If he was innocent, he should submit a petition in the proper course. . . . My brother did not relish this advice. "You do not know Kathiawad," he said,

[4] Pyarelal, *Mahatma Gandhi: The Early Phase* (Ahmedabad, 1965), I, 285–86.

[5] *Gandhi's Autobiography, or, The Story of My Experiments with Truth*, trans. from the Gujarati by Mahadev Desai (Washington, D.C., 1948), p. 123.

[6] *Ibid.*, pp. 123, 124.

"and you have yet to know the world. Only influence counts here. It is not proper for you, a brother, to shirk your duty, when you can clearly put in a good word about me to an officer you know."[7]

Mohandas felt he could not refuse his brother. At the same time he knew that he "had no right to approach the political agent and was fully conscious that he was compromising his self-respect." Yet he went, impelled by a sense of family obligation. Once he had stated his mission, Ollivant was immediately on his guard. " 'Surely you have not come here to abuse . . . our acquaintance, have you,' " was the message Mohandas read in Ollivant's manner. Gandhi continued. The political agent said he wished to hear no more; if his brother had anything to say, he should apply through proper channels. Gandhi persisted. "The *sahib* got up and said: 'You must go now.' " Again Mohandas took up his brother's brief. Ollivant, furious, ". . . called his peon and ordered him to show me the door. I was still hesitating when the peon came in, placed his hands on my shoulders and put me out of the room."[8] Humiliated, Gandhi wrote demanding that Ollivant make amends only to be told that "you are at liberty to proceed as you wish."[9] Desperate, Mohandas took advantage of the great Pherozeshah Mehta's presence in Rajkot, sending him a report of the events and seeking his advice. Mehta replied that if Gandhi expected to earn something and have an easy time in Rajkot, he should "tear up the note and pocket the insult."[10]

Gandhi found the advice "bitter as poison . . . but I had to swallow it." He vowed that he would never again place himself in such a false position and "since then I have never been guilty of a breach of that determination." This shock changed the course of his life by strengthening his concern for public as against familial obligation and driving him toward his South African decision.[11]

Gandhi approached the task of establishing a public ethic not only by ceaseless preaching and advice in particular cases but also by his own example and that of his immediate followers. His actions and deeds became anecdotal material for oral and written communication

[7] *Ibid.*, p. 124. [9] *Ibid.*

[8] *Ibid.*, p. 125. [10] *Ibid.*, p. 126. [11] *Ibid.*

and for parables that could be recounted to those who would listen as well as those who could read. As usual his wife and sons had to bear the brunt of the Mahatma's construction of models for virtuous action.

The particulars of some of the events involved will suggest their basic themes. When Gandhi left South Africa in 1901, the Indian community of Natal honored him in the customary manner by offering him many gifts, including a gold necklace for Kasturba worth fifty guineas. After the sleepless night that often accompanied Gandhi's struggles with an uneasy conscience, he determined to convert all the gifts into a public trust. They were, he concluded, a recognition of his public service. Kasturba resisted this conclusion: "I can understand your not permitting me to wear them. But what about my daughters-in-law? They will be sure to need them." When Gandhi proposed that she ask him for jewels when they were needed, she retorted, "Ask you? I know you by this time. You deprived me of my ornaments, you would not leave me in peace with them. Fancy you offering to get ornaments for the daughters-in-law. You, who would make *sadhus* of my boys. . . ." In the end, Gandhi reports, "I somehow succeeded in extorting a consent from her."[12]

When Gandhi first returned to India and established himself at Sabarmati Ashram, he placed Manilal, his second son, in charge of ashram funds that were the result of charitable gifts. When Manilal heard that Harilal, the unhappy first son, was without money in Calcutta, he borrowed money from the ashram to forward to his brother. Gandhi's discovery of the irregularity occasioned his banishing Manilal from the ashram.[13]

Once, also at Sabarmati Ashram, where a strong rule of simplicity prevailed, a thief carried off various articles, including two boxes of clothes belonging to Kasturba. "What I fail to understand," Gandhi observed at an ashram meeting called to consider the theft, "is how Ba [Kasturba] could at all have two boxes of clothes? For, she does not wear a different sari every day." Kasturba: "Rami and Manu [granddaughters] have lost their mother, as you know. Sometimes they come to stay with me. I kept away all the saris and pieces of

[12] *Ibid.*, pp. 270–72.

[13] Louis Fischer, *The Life of Mahatma Gandhi* (New York, 1962), p. 213.

khadi, given to me as presents from time to time, so that I can give them these things as gifts." Gandhi: "But we can not do that at all. Even the articles, given as gifts, if they are not of immediate use to the person to whom they are given, have to be deposited in the office."[14]

Because the ashram was supported by publicly subscribed funds, Gandhi made it a rule that all visitors, regardless of their connections to persons in the ashram, should pay for the expenses of their stay. This meant that Kasturba, whose strong sense of family connection and obligation attracted a good many visits, was required over her vehement protests and to her great embarrassment, to ask the manager to render bills to her relations.[15]

Incidents such as these became part of Gandhi lore, spreading from the press, the vernacular pages of *Navajivan* and the vernacular and English ones of Gandhi's autobiography, rippling outward from written sources to tales told in towns and villages by the widening circle of those for whom Gandhi's name and deeds were becoming legend. They illustrated that obligations to family and friends collided with the less familial, more public standard that Gandhi was attempting to erect in their place. Manilal did not embezzle funds for himself but to meet a brotherly obligation. Kasturba did not want the necklace or the collection of clothes for herself but to maintain the material and symbolic obligations of the family as a community. Her entirely unapologetic protests suggest that she knew her resistance was rooted in the morality of traditional obligations whereas his demands grew out of some alien vision.

The Gandhian norm for the conduct of public business translated this alien vision into a traditional idiom, dramatizing in the context of relations among family and friends what British public law, administration, and civic duty meant and required. By bringing the meaning of public obligation to those outside the small coterie of the English-educated, Gandhi helped place the idea and practice of civility on a more popular footing.[16]

[14] Mukulbhai Kalarthi (comp.), *Ba and Bapu,* pp. 27–28.

[15] *Ibid.,* p. 38.

[16] Edward Shils, "Ideology and Civility: On the Politics of Intellectuals," *Sewanee Review,* LXVI (Summer, 1958), 450–80.

The New Meaning of Old Paths

The ideas and techniques that Gandhi contributed to Indian nationalism were, in some ways, restatements of the truths he learned in his Gujarati childhood. That they were more than that, that they attained national, international, even historical, significance, is related to the nature of his return to them. He did not return unselfconsciously to wallow in the nostalgia of the familiar and the comfortable, the truths of sentiment unleavened by those of the conscience and the mind. Gandhi experienced and knew other alternatives. Many of his countrymen had also been touched in greater or lesser degree by their exposure to alien ideas and ways. He and they found inadequate the life path laid down by birth and family. Gandhi's return to that path, the path of home truths, grew out of his discomfort with the alternatives he tried, with his sense that he could not be himself by following them. This experience, too, coincided with that of many of his countrymen. But Gandhi found that the thoughts and emotions of his early days no longer fitted his sense of himself. Through an alien cultural experience, he won the freedom to choose, rather than be possessed by, the familiar, to reformulate and transform home truths. In settling with his own past, he gave familiar Indian ideas and practices new dignity and moral worth. He spoke to and increasingly persuaded not only those with backgrounds like his but also others that the self-definition and forms of protest and action that he new modeled were more worthy and better suited to them and their circumstances than the path of aggressive self-assertion.

The Gandhi who ate goat meat with Sheikh Mehtab because he envied his spirit and muscle went through a version of an experience common to several generations of Indians. They considered emulating the "mighty Englishman who ruled the Indian small" so that they might regain their dignity and independence. Gandhi, like others of his era, tried to strengthen himself by repairing to another cultural style. Instead of feeling more himself, he felt less so. He learned that for him integrity was tied to the culture of home and homeland, and the attempt failed.

Gandhi's return to vegetarianism, like his slow return from other attempts to acquire English manners and qualities, approximated the experiences of those unwilling or unable to manage the alternative model. When he turned to *satyagraha* and *ahimsa,* he revived the traditional view of courage, a view that carried with it commitments to non-violence, self-suffering, and self-restraint, qualities Englishmen had perceived differently and identified with cowardice. The path to courage that Gandhi showed his countrymen had fallen into disrepute among those affected by British power and ideas. He now gave it new life and meaning by making clear the exacting discipline it required in action and the kind of sacrifice and self-control it involved. Convincingly demonstrating its moral worthiness and practical worth, he was able to make the path to courage the path to popular nationalism. In the process of mastering his own fear and weakness, he reassured those generations near him that they need not fear or emulate those who had conquered them, that Macaulay and Strachey were wrong in believing them to be cowards. Nehru writes of Gandhi and India: "He had instilled courage and manhood in her people; . . . courage is the one sure foundation of character, he had said; without courage there is no morality, no religion, no love."[1]

Gandhi's political style, too, was a return to traditional modes. His asceticism had autobiographical origins in profound doubt about the permissibility of his masculine assertiveness. Its cultural origins lay in the enjoinment of lustfulness, of the rule of desire, in virtuous men, not least among whom were kings. Asceticism was also thought to bring with it a higher potency, an implication arising out of a theory of sexual hydrostatics reminiscent of Freudian sublimation theory. He who controls himself gains the strength to shape the environment. When Gandhi pursued the political goal of *swaraj* ("self-rule"), he meant to teach himself and Indians that only those who could rule themselves—in the sense of self-restraint—could rule

[1] Jawaharlal Nehru, *Freedom from Fear: Reflections on the Personality and Teachings of Gandhi* (Delhi, 1960), p. 12.

themselves—in the sense of controlling their political universe. His political effectiveness arose in part from the belief of those who observed his career that his self-control did indeed endow him with extraordinary powers. And it rested on the more practical fact that asceticism did bring him peace, not so much from leaping lusts, but from the recollection of the conflict between his own assertiveness and his duty to a father. The serenity he achieved by his asceticism was ultimately among his strongest assets as a leader of a mass movement that sometimes aroused strong feelings and evoked violent hatreds. It lay at the root of his capacity to act sensibly in a crisis, to keep himself from being thrown off stride by other people's hysteria. His serenity conveyed to others, who often were hysterical, the reminder that reasonable conduct could be recaptured in the midst of boundless and irrational chaos. Especially when tested in the communal blood baths of the forties, it lay at the basis of his capacity to make men act as much as possible like men rather than driven creatures.

INDEX

Index